# THE
# OFFICIAL
# AMAZON SELLER
# CLASSROOM IN A BOOK
# VOLUME III

# THE
# OFFICIAL
# AMAZON SELLER
# CLASSROOM IN A BOOK

## VOLUME III

## DREW BERRY

## Legal Notice:

ISBN-13: 9781705625699

## Disclaimer:

The information provided herein is stated to be truthful and consistent, in that any liability, in terms of inattention or otherwise, by any usage or abuse of policies, processes, or directions contained within is the solitary and utter responsibility of the recipient reader. Under no circumstances will any legal responsibility or blame be held against the publisher for any reparation, damages, or monetary loss due to the information herein, either directly or indirectly.

Please note that the content within this document is for educational and informational purposes only. Every attempt has been made to provide accurate, up to date, and reliable complete information. No warranties of any kind are expressed or implied. By reading this document, the reader agrees that under no circumstances is the author or publisher responsible for any losses, direct or indirect, which are incurred as a result of the information contained within this document, including, but not limited to; errors, omissions, or inaccuracies.

## Special Thanks:

Special thanks to the developers at Amazon, Google, Microsoft, Helium 10, and Alibaba for providing the necessary software.

This book is dedicated to my readers. May you each find great success as an Amazon Seller!

# Table Of Contents

*<u>Note:</u> Volume III is a continuance of "The Official Amazon Seller Classroom In A Book" series therefore it begins where Volume II concluded which is Chapter 10.

# Chapter 10:

# Opening A Business Bank Account & Acquiring A Business Credit Card:

An integral aspect of being an Amazon Seller is keeping track of your incoming and outgoing financial revenue. You will be paying suppliers through (B2B) Marketplace platforms, such as, Alibaba as well as receiving payments for your product listing sales from Amazon on a bi-monthly basis all of which will be conducted through the use of a bank account. Although you do have the ability to create and operate your Amazon Seller Central account with a personal checking account I do not recommend doing this and instead advise opting for a business bank account. Running your business through the use of a business bank in contrast to a personal checking account is beneficial for several reasons.

**Purpose & Benefits Of Opening A Business Bank Account Versus A Personal Checking Account:**

- Whether you formed a Sole Proprietor, Partnership, (C-Corp) Corporation, or (S-Corp) Corporation if money is being transacted then you are required by the (IRS) to have a business bank account by the same name as your incorporated entity.

- You are able to keep your personal checking account finances separate from your business checking account finances which prevents confusion when performing either personal or business banking bookkeeping tasks. Ultimately, a well kempt personal checking account and business bank account will make the task of preparing and filing your annual Federal and State taxes much easier to perform.

- You will be utilizing your business bank account for numerous transactions which makes the threat of fraudulent activity occurring a higher threat. If you were utilizing your personal checking account as your business bank account then the criminal would simultaneously have access to all of your finances. Ultimately, by keeping your personal finances separate from your business finances you tremendously reduce the risk of this scenario occurring.

- Creates a sense of professionalism with your (B2B) suppliers through marketplaces, such as, Alibaba, since the name on the bank account that you utilize to make your purchases will be that of your business.

- As your Amazon Seller business prospers through the use of your business bank account you will start to build your credit with your bank of choice which means that if you ever need a loan from them you can easily prove that your business is profitable. Ultimately, having a business bank account separate from your personal checking account with all of your business finances organized, tracked, and accounted for will make the process of applying for and receiving a loan much easier to perform.

- You can easily track your business related transactions Online via mobile banking.

## The Following List Of Items Are Required To Open A Business Bank Account As An Amazon Seller:

- One Form Of Identification: Driver's License, Identification Card, or Passport
- (EIN) (Chapter 6)
- Articles Of Incorporation (Chapter 6)
- Business Or Home Address
- Working Phone Line
- Your Secondary Professional Email Address (Chapter 7)

*Note: Although the list above contains the primary items you will need to open most e-commerce focused business bank accounts I recommend calling the bank of your choice and asking them exactly what they require for account creation prior to driving to their location. Depending on your state and region of residence you may be required to obtain a business license and show proof of your business address in order to open your business account.

## Tips On Choosing The Right Bank For Your Business Needs:

- Spend some time conducting research Online of the different banks in your state and region that offer business bank accounts.

You will find that some banks offer either one or more of the following attributes:

- Promotional initial sign up deals.
- $0 monthly fees.
- Free business banking with certain amount of monthly transactions performed.
- No minimum account balances.
- Free (ATM) withdraws.
- Cashback on debit card purchases.
- Savings business bank accounts with gainable interest.

- Discuss your business banking needs with the bank that you already utilize for your personal checking account.

- You can opt for a non-branch online-only bank, such as, (TIAA) at www.tiaabank.com.

## Importance Of Acquiring A Business Credit Card:

Creating an Amazon Seller Central account requires you to have a credit card not a debit card. Although you can use a personal credit card to perform this task I recommend acquire and utilizing a business credit card for your Amazon Seller purposes. This is another way to keep your personal and business finances separate. Ultimately, by conducting business in this manner, you can simultaneously protect your personal finances, build your credit score under your entity name, and easily track your business related costs, such as, your ($39.99) monthly fee for retailing on Amazon.

## Tips On Choosing & Utilizing The Right Business Credit Card For Your Needs:

- Spend some time conducting research Online to locate the best business credit card.

## I Recommend Locating A Business Credit Card That Offers Either One Or More Of The Following:

- o 0% APR for the first year.
- o A low (APR).
- o No annual fee.
- o A % of cash back when purchases are made.
- o Introductory cash bonus for acquiring the credit card.

- I recommend utilizing your business credit card for any membership or service that you subscribe to as an Amazon Seller. By conducting your business in this manner, you can consolidate all of your membership fees into one easily trackable monthly payment.

## Subscription Services To Consolidate Onto Your Business Credit Card:

- o Microsoft Software Subscription
- o Helium 10
- o Go-Daddy Website Hosting Fees
- o Adobe Illustrator
- o Amazon Seller Central: Professional Selling Plan: ($39.99/Month)

*Opening a business bank account is another significant essential milestone to becoming and remaining a successful Amazon Seller.

# To-Do List Chapter 10:

- Research & Choose A Bank To Open Your Business Bank Account.
- Open Your Business Bank Account.
- Obtain Online/Mobile Access To Your Business Bank Account.
- Obtain A Business Credit Card.
- If You Are Charged A Fee For Having A Business Bank Account Download Your Monthly Invoice & Store It In Your Microsoft Word Document, Titled, "Amazon Business Invoices," From Section 3.11.
- Record The Monthly Business Bank Account Fee Into Your Microsoft Excel Spreadsheet Titled, "Amazon Business Finances," From Section 3.11.

# Chapter 11:

## Creating Your Amazon Seller Central Account, Signing Into It, & Understanding How To Navigate Through It:

**Seller Central:** https://sellercentral.amazon.com

Amazon Seller Central is an online user-friendly platform created for the sole purpose of building, posting, advertising, and managing product listings on Amazon for third-party Amazon Sellers.

**To Create Your Amazon Seller Central Account & Sign Into It, follow the instructional steps included with the labeled images below:**

**Step #1:** Choose a membership type and plan:

| Plan Type | Price |
|---|---|
| Individual Selling Plan | $0/Month<br>$1.00 Per Unit Charge For Each Sale Made |
| Professional Selling Plan | $39.99/Month<br>$0 Per Unit Charge For Each Sale Made<br>*First Month Is Free Of Charge |

**\*Note:** As you can observe from the chart below the best option for Amazon Sellers intending on selling more than (40) units per month is the "Professional Selling Plan."

**Example: Individual Seller vs Professional Seller:**

Per say, we had two Amazon Sellers who each separately sold (1000) units over a one month period of time. One Seller is signed up for the "Individual Selling Plan" and the other is signed up for the Professional Selling Plan."

## Compare & Contrast The Chart Below:

| Plan Type | Sales Made | Price Paid To Amazon |
|---|---|---|
| Individual Seller | 1000 | $1/Unit=$1000 |
| Professional Seller | 1000 | $0/Unit=$39.99 |

## Step #2:

### Make Sure You Have The Following Items Readily Available:

- Secondary Professional Email Address (Chapter 7)
- Credit Card (Not A Debit Card)
- Smartphone With Cell Service (Ability To Receive Text Messages)
- Business Address
- Valid Government Issued Passport, Driver's License, Or Identification Card
- Primary Company Name (Chapter 5)
- Company Website Address (Chapter 7)
- USA (EIN) Tax Identification Number (Chapter 6)
- Business Bank Account Number (Chapter 10)
- Business Bank Account (9) Digit Routing Number (Chapter 10)
- Your Most Recent Bank Or Credit Card Statement

**Step #3:** Navigate https://sellercentral.amazon.com from within the Google Chrome Web Browser.

**Step #4:** Using your mouse, left-click and release on the "Register now" navigational task button:

**Step #5:** Using your mouse, left-click and release on the "Start selling" navigational task button:

**Step #6:** Using your mouse, left-click and release on the "Create your Amazon account" navigational task button:

## Step #7:

### You Must Provide:

- Your Full Name Exactly As It Is Printed On Your Driver License Or Identification Card
- Your Secondary Professional Email Address (Chapter 7)
- A Memorable Password

❖ After you have filled in the required information, using your mouse, left-click and release on the yellow "Next" navigational task button:

**Step #8:** Amazon will now require you check your email to obtain an account creation verification (OTP) pin number. As you can observe in the screenshot below, once you check your email and locate the (6) digit pin you will navigate back to the Amazon Seller Central account page and enter the (OTP) number in the section provided by Amazon. Then using your mouse, left-click and release on the "Verify" navigational task button:

**Step #9:** You will first make sure that you have the required information listed on the webpage. You will then enter the Legal Name of your business entity and check the box agreeing to Amazon's terms and conditions. Then using your mouse, left-click and release on the "Next" navigational task button:

## Step #10:

### You Must Provide:

o The Address Your Business Entity Is Legally Registered Under (Chapter 6)
o Your Primary Company Name (Chapter 5)
o Your Company Website (URL) (Chapter 7)
o Your Valid Working Cell Number

*After you have enter the required information you will be need to receive your Amazon Seller Central account verification through either an SMS (Text Message) or via phone call. After you choose your preferred pin receival method, using your mouse, left-click and release on the "Send SMS or Call Now" navigational task button:

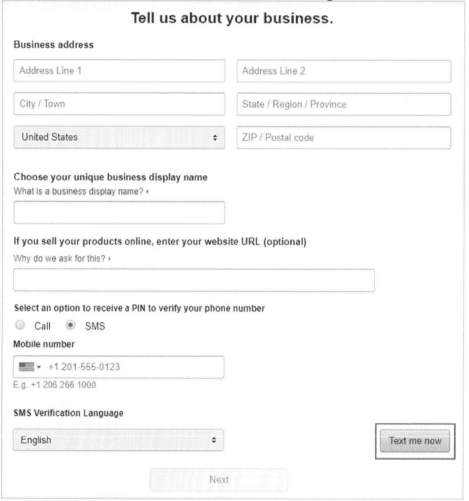

**Step #11:** If you opted for text message verification you will now enter the (6) digit pin sent you via SMS. Then using your mouse, left-click and release on the "Verify" navigational task button:

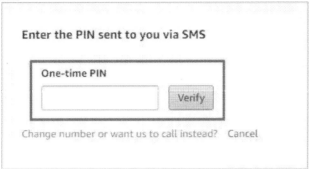

**Step #12:** You will now observe that you have successfully verified your account. Then using your mouse, left-click and release on the "Next" navigational task button:

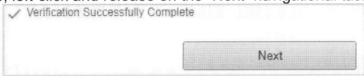

**Step #13:** Using your mouse, left-click and release on the "Select" navigational task button to choose the market (Your Country Of Residence) that you will be retailing in:

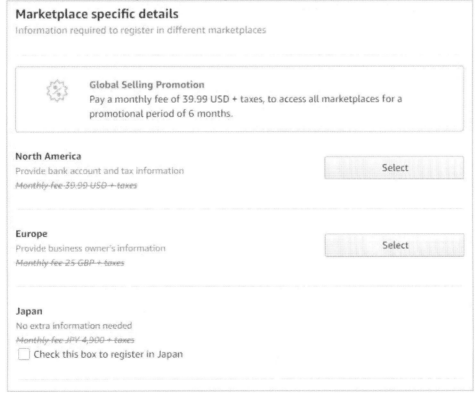

**Step #14:** You will enter your name and your business bank account information (Routing Number Account Number). Then using your mouse, left-click and release on the "Next" navigational task button:

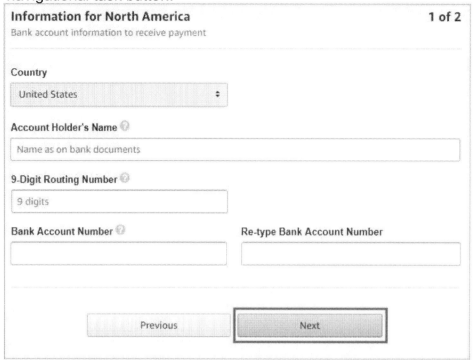

**Step #15:** You will now be required to conduct an online tax interview with Amazon.

*To begin the tax interview, using your mouse, left-click and release on yellow "Start" navigational task button:

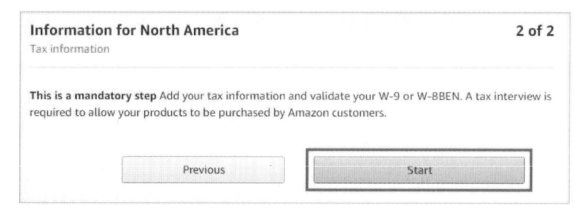

## Step #16:

### You Will Now Choose:

- o Whether You Are An Individual Or A Business Entity
- o Whether You Reside In The USA
- o Your Tax Classification (Entity Type You Formed, Chapter 6)

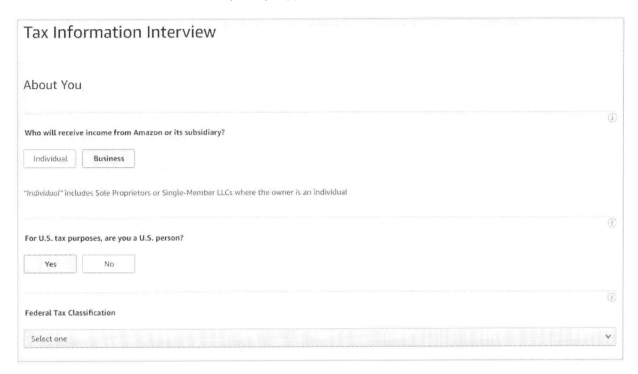

Tax Information Interview

About You

Who will receive income from Amazon or its subsidiary?

Individual  |  **Business**

*"Individual"* includes Sole Proprietors or Single-Member LLCs where the owner is an individual

For U.S. tax purposes, are you a U.S. person?

Yes  |  No

Federal Tax Classification

Select one ⌄

## Step #17:

### You Must Provide:

- o  Your Name
- o  The Name Of Your Business Entity As It Is Legally Registered (Chapter 6)
- o  The Address Your Business Entity Is Legally Registered Under (Chapter 6)
- o  Your Business (EIN) (Chapter 6)

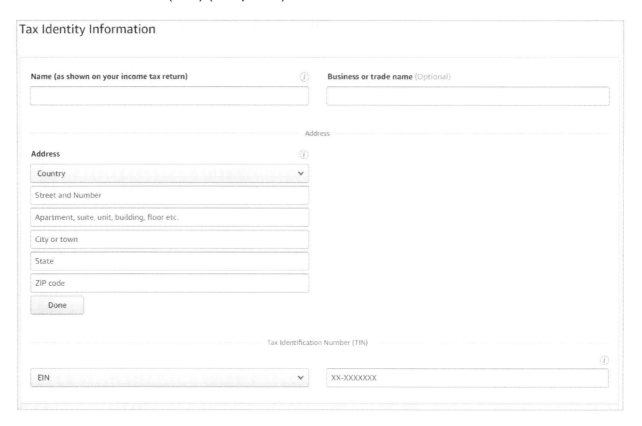

**Step #18:** Using your mouse, left-click and release on the "Continue" navigational task button:

**Step #19:** You will now electronically "Sign and Submit" your contract stating the information you provided is true and correct:

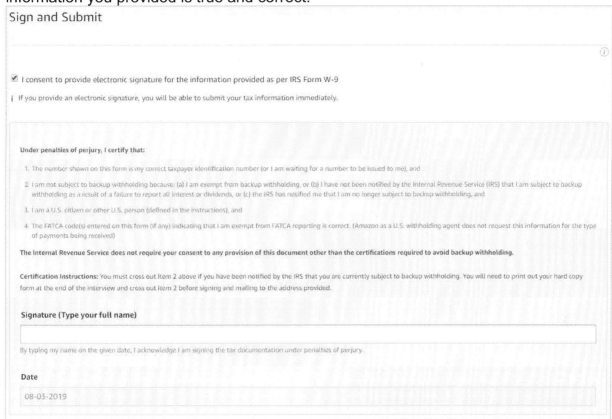

**Step #20:** Using your mouse, left-click and release on the "Save and Preview" navigational task button:

Save and Preview

**Step #21:** I recommend reviewing your information to make sure it has been correctly entered. Then using your mouse, left-click and release on the "Submit Form" navigational task button:

Submit Form

**Step #22:** As you can observe in the screenshot below, it will take time for Amazon to validate your tax information.

　　　*Using your mouse, left-click and release on the "Exit Interview" navigational task button to proceed with your account creation:

**Step #23:**

### You Must Provide:

　o　Your Primary Company Name (Chapter 5)

*Note: Upon entering your primary company name Amazon's system will instantly let you know whether or not your preferred primary company name is available. If you did the proper research discussed within Chapter 5 no issues should arise when performing this task. If your primary company name is unavailable I recommend either changing the name entirely to prevent confusion with consumers or if you do not already have it adding an INC. (Incorporated) to the end of the title.

### Example Of Adding INC. To An Unavailable Primary Company Name:

- Primary Company Name: "UP" Is Unavailable
- Change The Primary Company Name To: UP INC.

## You Must State That You:

- ○ Have or will have (UPCs) to create your product listings (Chapter 9)
- ○ You are the owner of the company and the brands you will be retailing on Amazon
- ○ You have or will have legally registered trademarks for your primary company name, brand name, and brand logos (Chapters 5 & 9)

**Step #24:** Enter your credit card (Debit Card Unacceptable) information:

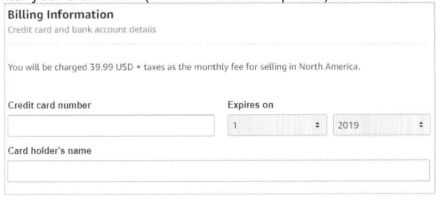

**Step #25:** Using your mouse, left-click and release on the "Next" navigational task button:

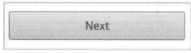

**Step #26:** Enter your Passport, Driver's License, or Identification Card information:

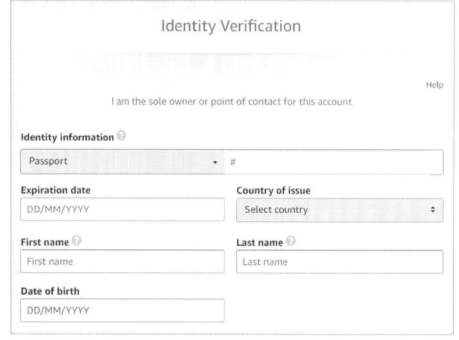

**Step #27:** Using your mouse, left-click and release on the "Submit" navigational task button:

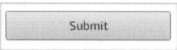

**Step #28:** You will now be required to upload a copy of your identification document. To do so, using your mouse, left-click on the "Upload front side" navigational task button. You will then repeat these steps for the back side of your identification document:

*Note: You can either scan your document into your computer using your printer or opt to take an image utilizing your smartphone then send that to yourself via email and upload the image into your computer's hard drive.

**Step #29:** You will now be required to either upload your most current bank or credit card statement:

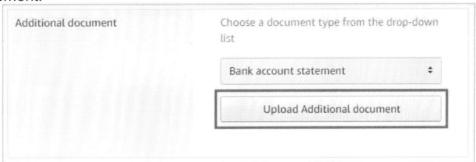

**Step #30:** Once you are finished uploading the proper documentation, using your mouse, left-click and release on the "Submit" navigational task button:

**Step #31:** You must now wait for Amazon to verify your information which can take up to (2) business days, but typically takes no more than (12) hours.

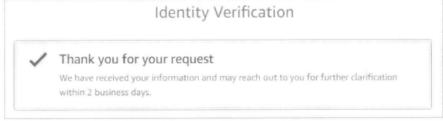

## To Track Your Amazon Seller Central Application Status:

- You can periodically log into your Amazon Seller Central account to observe if the account creation process has progressed and you have access to the Selling platform.
- Look within your inbox for emails received from Amazon Seller Central.

## Overview Of Navigating Through Amazon Seller Central:

amazon seller central

**Amazon Seller Central Icon:** This icon can be utilized to quickly navigate back to the homepage from any section of your Amazon Seller Central account.

**Notifications Icon:** This icon allows quick access view to any important messages you have received through your Amazon Seller Central account.

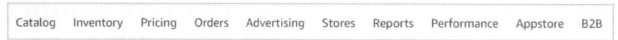

**Taskbar:** The taskbar contains the primary tools you will utilize as an Amazon Seller.

## From The Taskbar You Can Perform The Following List Of Tasks:

- Build your product listings.
- Manage your inventory.
- Manage your product listing price points.
- Manage your customer orders.
- Create, run, & manage your Amazon product listing marketing campaigns.
- Enroll your product (SKUs) into the (ERP) Early Reviewer Program.
- Enroll your products into Brand Registry.
- Create & design your Amazon Storefronts.
- Run reports.
- Track various aspects of your overall performance metrics as an Amazon Seller.
- Purchase Amazon Seller related software applications.
- Navigate to (B2B) central.

**Marketplace Navigator:** If you retail your products in other countries you can quickly switch to the Amazon Marketplace of your choice through utilization of this navigator drop down list icon.

**Search Bar:** You can utilize the quick answer search bar to ask questions you have regarding tasks you need to perform as an Amazon Seller.

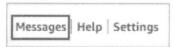

**Messages:** The "Message" task button is utilized to navigate you to your message center where you can read through your notifications and directly correspond with buyers that require a response.

**Help:** The "Help" task button is utilized to navigate you to the help center where you can learn and receive guidance on how to properly perform tasks as an Amazon Seller.

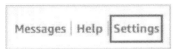

**Settings:** The "Settings" icon is utilized to generate a navigational task button settings menu.

**From The Settings Menu You Can Perform The Following List Of Tasks:**

- Sign out of your Amazon Seller Central account.
- View & alter your account info.
- View & alter your notification preferences.
- View & alter your login settings.
- View & alter your product return settings.
- View & alter your product gift wrap settings.
- View & alter your shipping settings.
- View & alter your tax settings.
- View & alter your user permissions.
- View & alter your company info & policies.
- View & alter your (FBA) settings.

**Widgets:** The Rest Of The Amazon Seller Central Marketplace Platform Is Comprised Of The Following List Of Statistical Data, Informational, & Navigational Widgets.

Your Orders     •••

**Your Orders:** This widget provides a quick overview observation of information regarding your (FBM) & (FBA) product listing orders.

Performance     •••

**Performance:** This widget provides a quick overview observation of your customer feedback, buyer messages, and account health metrics.

Seller Forums     •••

**Seller Forums:** This widget provides a quick overview of third-party seller conversational forums that are currently taking place on the Amazon Marketplace.

| News | ... |
|---|---|

**News:** This widget notifies of you of new changes made by Amazon in regard to retailing on the Amazon Marketplace.

| Getting Started | ... |
|---|---|

**Getting Started:** This widget can be utilized to learn how to properly execute various tasks on the Amazon Marketplace.

| Amazon Selling Coach | ... |
|---|---|

**Amazon Selling Coach:** This widget offers you various tips, strategies, and recommendations you can utilize to make your business on the Amazon Marketplace run smoothly and be profitable.

| Amazon Business | ... |
|---|---|

**Amazon Business:** This widget allows you to quickly and easily manage your Amazon Business certifications, profile, pricing, & documents.

| Payments Summary | ... |
|---|---|

**Payments Summary:** This widget provides a quick overview observation of your Amazon transferred fund amounts.

| Manage Your Case Log | ... |
|---|---|

**Manage Your Case Log:** This widget provides quick navigation to the page containing all past or current cases you have opened with Amazon.

| Sales Summary | ... |
|---|---|

**Sales Summary:** This widget provides a quick overview observation of your (7), (15) & (30) day product listing sales data.

| List globally | ... |
|---|---|

**List Globally:** If you sell within several Amazon Marketplaces this widget provides a quick overview observation of your active product listing metrics.

**Seller Poll:** Through the use of quick answer questionnaires Amazon utilizes this widget to ask your personal opinion about various characteristics in regard to utilizing the Amazon Marketplace.

Although I will be teaching you how to utilize specific features of Amazon Seller Central, before forging ahead with the following chapters and the tutorials they contain, I recommend first familiarizing yourself with the Amazon Marketplace platform by clicking through each section of your account.

### Utilizing The Amazon Seller Smartphone App:

Now that you have created your Amazon Seller Central account you can opt to utilize the Amazon Seller smartphone app that you downloaded in Chapter 3, Section 3.13. When you sign in on your smartphone the app automatically syncs your accounts which allows you to perform various Amazon Seller tasks directly from your portable device. The Amazon Seller app makes working while traveling feasible, simple, and manageable.

*Seller Central account creation is another significant essential milestone to becoming and remaining a successful Amazon Seller.

### To-Do List Chapter 11:

- Create Your Amazon Seller Central Account.
- Sign Into Amazon Seller Central.
- Learn How To Navigate Through Amazon Seller Central.
- Sign Into & Sync Your Amazon Seller Central Account Via The Smartphone App.
- Download Your Monthly Invoice For Your $39.99 Professional Selling & Store It In Your Microsoft Word Document, Titled, "Amazon Business Invoices," From Section 3.11.
- Record The $39.99 Monthly Amazon Selling Plan Fee Into Your Microsoft Excel Spreadsheet Titled, "Amazon Business Finances," From Section 3.11.

# Chapter 12:

## Granting Helium 10 Third-Party (MWS) Access To Your Amazon Seller Central Account:

When you use third-party software, such as Helium 10, to assist you in operating your business Amazon requires you to grant the company's tools (MWS) Marketplace Web Service access to your Amazon Seller Central account. Please be aware, that by granting Helium 10 (MWS) access to your Amazon Seller Central account you are not giving Helium 10 user access to your Amazon Seller Central account. You are solely granting the permissions required by Amazon that allow the software provided by Helium 10 to function when you use it to perform the particular tasks the tools were designed to accomplish. Furthermore, you can revoke your (MWS) granted permissions at any time you choose from within your Helium 10 user profile account settings.

**The Following List Of Helium 10 Software Tools Require (MWS) Access To Your Amazon Seller Central Account To Effectively Function:**

- Keyword Tracker
- Alerts
- Inventory Protector
- Refund Genie
- Profits
- Follow-Up

**To Grant Helium 10 (MWS) Access To Your Amazon Seller Central Account, follow the instructional steps included with the labeled images below:**

**Step #1:** Navigate to www.helium10.com from within the Google Chrome Web Browser, sign into your account, and be sure that you are subscribed to Helium 10's Platinum, Diamond, or Elite membership plan as was discussed in Chapter 4.

**Step #2:** Using your mouse, left-click and release on your profile user icon located on the top right-hand side of Helium 10's homepage to generate a list of navigational tasks you can perform:

**Step #3:** Using your mouse, left-click and release on your user profile icon to navigate to your Helium 10 account settings:

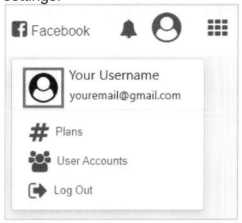

**Step #4:** Using your mouse, scroll down your account settings page and locate the section titled "Helium 10 Connectors":

Helium 10 Connectors

**Step #5:** Using your mouse, left-click and release on the "Show me what to do" button to generate a list of navigational tasks:

Amazon MWS (Seller Central) - North America (US/CA/MX/BR)
Show me what to do

**Step #6:** Using your mouse, left-click and release on the "Authenticate Your Seller Account" button to navigate to the Amazon (MWS) authentication webpage:

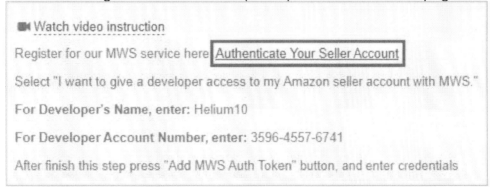

**Step #7:** You will observe that both the "Developer's Name: Helium 10" and **"Developer ID: 3596-4557-6741"** have been automatically entered. Using your mouse, left-click and release on the "Next" navigational task button:

**Step #8:** Using your mouse, check the box and agree to allow Helium 10 (MWS) access to your Amazon Seller Central account. Then using your mouse, left-click and release on the "Next" navigational task button:

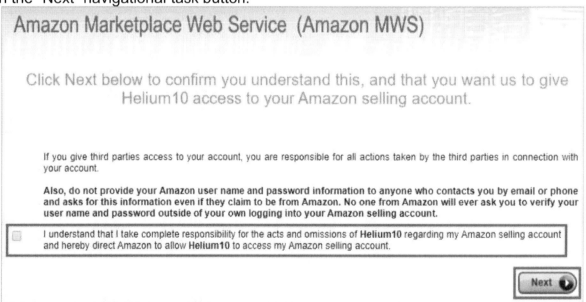

**Step #9:** You will now observe that you have granted Helium 10 (MWS) access to your Amazon Seller Central account. Furthermore, you will observe a list containing your Seller ID, Marketplace ID, and (MWS) Authorization Token, which you will be utilizing in the following final Step #12, therefore I recommend printing this page for further reference:

**Step #10:** Navigate back to your helium 10 account settings page as you did within the previous Step #'s (1-3).

**Step #11:** Using your mouse, scroll down your account settings page and locate the section titled "Helium 10 Connectors." Then using your mouse, left-click and release on the "Add Token" navigational task button:

**Step #12:** Enter your Amazon Seller ID and (MWS) Auth Token that you received within the previous Step #9:

**<u>To Grant Helium 10 (MWS) Access To Your Amazon Marketplace (PPC) Ad Campaigns, follow the instructional steps included with the labeled images below:</u>**

**<u>Step #1:</u>** Navigate to www.helium10.com from within the Google Chrome Web Browser and be sure to be subscribed to Helium 10's Platinum, Diamond, or Elite membership plan as was discussed in Chapter 4.

**<u>Step #2:</u>** Using your mouse, left-click and release on your profile user icon located on the top right-hand side of Helium 10's homepage to generate a list of navigational tasks you can perform:

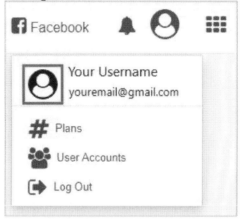

**<u>Step #3:</u>** Using your mouse, left-click and release on your user profile icon to navigate to your Helium 10 account settings:

**<u>Step #4:</u>** Using your mouse, scroll down your account settings page and locate the section titled "Helium 10 Connectors":

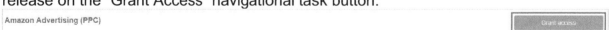

**<u>Step #5:</u>** Locate the "Amazon Advertising (PPC)." Then using your mouse, left-click and release on the "Grant Access" navigational task button:

Amazon Advertising (PPC)　　　　　　　　　　　　　　　　　　　　　　　Grant access

**Step #6:** You will now be required to sign into Amazon Seller Central account by entering the information you utilized to create your account within Chapter 11:

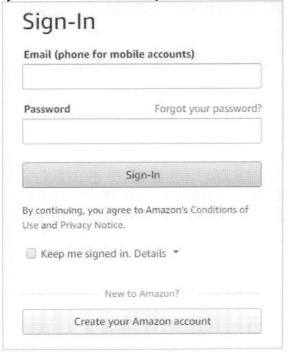

**Step #7:** Using your mouse, left-click and release on the "Allow" task button to grant Helium 10 (MWS) access to your Amazon Marketplace (PPC) advertising campaigns:

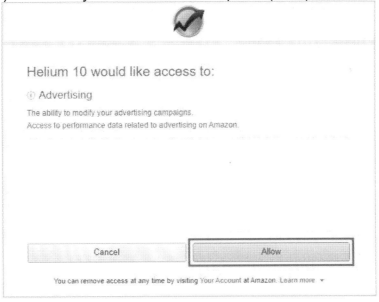

**\*Note:** Now that you have granted Helium 10 (MWS) access to your Amazon Seller Central account you can opt to receive profit performance reports, tailored product listing change alerts, and keyword tracking notifications via email from Helium 10.

**To Receive Profit Performance Reports, Tailored Product Listing Change Alerts, & Keyword Tracking Notifications Via Email From Helium 10, follow the instructional steps included with the labeled images below:**

**Step #1:** Navigate to www.helium10.com from within the Google Chrome Web Browser.

**Step #2:** Using your mouse, left-click and release on your profile user icon located on the top right-hand side of Helium 10's homepage to generate a list of navigational tasks you can perform:

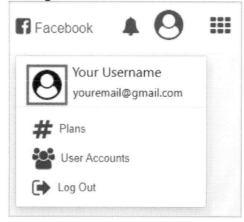

**Step #3:** Using your mouse, left-click and release on your user profile icon to navigate to your Helium 10 account settings:

**Step #4:** Using your mouse, scroll down your account settings page and locate the section titled "Application Preferences":

**Step #5:** As you can observe in the screenshot below, you can opt to receive Daily, Weekly, and Monthly "Profit" performance reports via email from Helium 10:

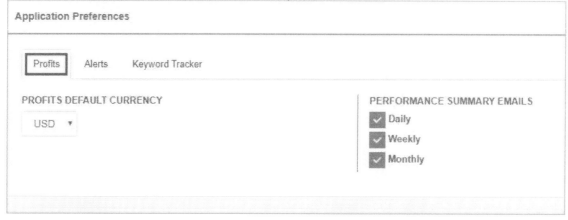

**Step #6:** As you can observe in the screenshot below, you can opt to receive tailored "Alerts" via email from Helium 10 when specific changes occur on your Amazon product listings:

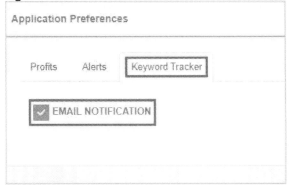

**Step #7:** As you can observe in the screenshot below, you can opt to receive notifications via email from Helium 10 when changes occur in reference to specific keywords you are tracking:

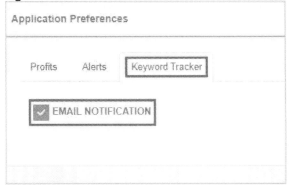

*Granting Helium 10 (MWS) access to your Seller Central account is another significant essential milestone to becoming and remaining a successful Amazon Seller.

## To-Do List Chapter 12:

- Grant Helium 10 (MWS) Access To Your Amazon Seller Central Account.
- Grant Helium 10 (MWS) Access To Your Amazon Marketplace (PPC) Advertising Campaigns.
- Navigate To Your Helium 10 Account Settings & Locate The "Application Preferences" Section To Receive Profit Performance Reports, Tailored Product Listing Change Alerts, & Keyword Tracking Notifications Via Email From Helium 10.

# Chapter 13:

## The Importance Of Having High-Resolution Product Images For Your Amazon Listings & How To Obtain Them:

A fundamental aspect of building exceedingly optimized Amazon product listings relies heavily on having professional high-resolution images of your merchandise for consumers to view prior to purchase. As an Amazon Seller it is imperative to understand that customers shopping on Amazon are doing so solely with their eyes in contrast to being in a brick and mortar store where they can personally pick up, touch, and truly feel the texture of a product. By having remarkably rich detailed product imagery shot from several angles for the buyer to click through you can utilize their eyes to stimulate their imagination and give them the sense that they are holding the merchandise in their hands. Ultimately, aside from the text within your product listings, your product images are your only opportunity to showcase your merchandise to a consumer prior to purchase therefore they must be exceptionally exquisite and attractive.

### Amazon's General (TOS) For Product Images:

- Acceptable forms of images are JPEG, TIFF, & GIF file format.
- The images must be a dimension of at least (1000) pixels in height or width.
- The color profile of the images must be sRGB or CMYK.
- Your product listing can have up to **(9)** product images.

    - **(1)** Primary Lead Product Image
    - **(8)** Additional Product Images

The first image the consumer will observe when searching for a product to purchase is known as your primary lead Amazon product listing image. This initial key image is your opportunity to attract the customer's attention as well as introduce your company, brand, and the merchandise you carry. The ultimate goal of your primary lead image is to feature your product, convey the message that you carry high-quality merchandise, draw the customer into your product listing, and convert them into a buyer.

## Amazon's (TOS) For The Primary Lead Product Image:

- The image must be of the actual product not an illustration or drawing.
- The image must be of professional grade.
- The image must be professionally lit.
- The image must be in focus.
- The image must fill at least **(85%)** of the frame.
- The entire product must be in the frame.
- The image must not contain text or graphics: (Primary Company Name, Brand Name, or Brand Logo unless printed on the product itself)
- No images showing the product in use are allowed.
- Product individual packaging is allowed but not recommended.
- The image must not contain a background or environment.
- The background color must be white.

**Image:** A professional grade high-resolution primary lead product listing image in accordance with Amazon's (TOS):

ICONIC Vintage Polarized
Sunglasses
★★★★☆ ˅ 446

$16⁹⁹ $29.99

FREE Shipping on orders over $25
shipped by Amazon

# Amazon's (TOS) For The (8) Additional Product Images:

- The image must be of the actual product not an illustration or drawing.
- The image must be of professional grade.
- The image must be professionally lit.
- The images must be in focus.
- The images must fill at least **(85%)** of the frame.
- The entire product must be in the frame.
- The image can contain text or graphics: (Primary Company Name, Brand Name, or Brand Logo)
- Images showing the product in use are allowed.
- Product individual packaging is allowed and recommended.
- The images can contain a background or environment.
- Images that are close-up showing specific product attributes are allowed.

## Pro Tips:

**1)** I recommend utilizing product images that are no less than **(1500x1500)** pixels in dimension. A high pixel dimension results in concise, clear, crisp, and clean images.

**2)** I do not recommend utilizing product images provided from your supplier, the Alibaba Marketplace, or websites as they are typically lower quality and will most likely not meet the requirements of Amazon's specific (TOS).

**3)** To gain traction, create visibility, and ultimately have your brand be recognizable on Amazon your product listing images must be comparable or better than that of your competitors therefore I recommend investigating their listings and observing the quality of their images. You must remember that consumers shopping on Amazon are doing so with their eyes therefore the chance that they would opt to buy a product with lower quality images versus one with higher quality images is very slim.

**4)** To create perceived value, I recommend having one of your additional product images contain the product and its individual packaging or simply your product's individual packaging. I suggest making this image the second in your list directly following your primary lead product listing image.

<u>**Image:**</u> An additional product image containing individual packaging:

**5)** I recommend having one of your additional product images display your product from different angles ultimately giving the consumer a (360) degree view.

<u>**Image:**</u> An additional product image containing different views and angles of the merchandise:

**6)** When applicable I recommend having one of your additional product images illustrate the exact dimensions and state the weight of your product. These types of informative graphics can easily be created in Adobe Illustrator.

**Image:** An additional product image containing the exact dimensions and weight of the product:

**7)** I recommend having one of your additional images be a lifestyle photograph with a background that helps to convey the actual size of the product to the consumer.

**Image:** An additional product image containing a lifestyle photograph with a background that helps convey the size of the merchandise:

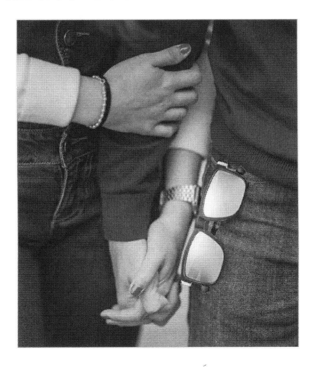

**8)** I recommend having one of your additional product images be a lifestyle photograph that demonstrates the product in use and its key features.

**Image:** An additional product image containing a lifestyle photograph of the product in use:

**9)** I recommend having one of your additional product images contain the product, state its special attributes, and show close-up shots of important features accompanied by explanatory text. These types of informative graphics can easily be created in Adobe Illustrator.

**Image:** An additional product image featuring the product's key attributes:

# (2) Methods Of Obtaining Professional Product Images:

## Method #1:

- Shoot your product photography yourself which will require studio grade photography equipment:

**Required Equipment For Shooting Professional Product Photography:**

**1) Camera:** I recommend purchasing a professional (DSLR) single reflex lens camera that preferably shoots both images and video.

**I Recommend:**

**Type:** (DSLR) Nikon D7500
**Specs:**
- 20.9 Megapixels
- ISO: 100-51,200
- Ability To Take 4K UHD Video

**Price:**
($899.95) Camera Body Only
($1499.95) Camera Body With 16-80mm Lens
**Location:** www.nikonusa.com

**\*Note:** I recommend researching and purchasing the Nikon D7200 or Nikon D5600 as a kit which includes the camera body, required lenses, and a tripod on www.amazon.com. The pricing is much more reasonable on Amazon in contrast to www.nikonusa.com.

**2) Tripod:** To shoot professional product images successfully without blur you will require a (DSLR) tripod for your camera.

**I Recommend:**

**Type:** Neewer Carbon Fiber Tripod With Portable Carry/Storage Bag Included
**Specs:**
- ¼ Inch Quick Shoe Plate
- 2 In 1: (Can be used as a tripod or monopod)

**Price:** ($99.99)
**Location:** www.amazon.com

**3) Lighting Setup:** To obtain professional lighting for your product images you will require a light kit setup containing at least two photography studio grade lights.

**I Recommend:**

**Type:** Elinchrom D-Lite RX 4, 4 Softbox To Go Kit
**Price:** ($729.99)
**Location:** www.adorama.com or www.amazon.com

**4) Studio:** An Area To Shoot The Product Images With A White Background:

## (2) Options For Creating A Photography Studio Setup:

**Option #1:** You can purchase a tabletop studio.

**Type:** Modahaus Tabletop Studio Pro 400
**Specs:**
- White Background

**Price:** ($94.83)
**Location:** www.modahaus.com

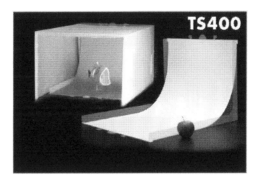

**Option #2:** You can easily build a custom tabletop studio similar to the image above.

**Materials required:**

- (2-4) Metal Clamps
- A Roll Of White Craft Paper
- A Chair Or Table

## (2) Options For Amazon Sellers On A Tight Budget:

**Option #1:** If you live in a city there may be a place that allows you to rent the equipment you require to shoot your product photography. If you are attempting to utilize this method I recommend performing an Internet search for photography equipment rentals in your area.

**Option #2:** Although I do not recommend it, If you are on a tight budget you can opt to shoot your images with a smartphone. If you must utilize this method I suggest purchasing and equipping a lens setup to your smartphone.

### Smartphones Recommend For Product Photography:

- Samsung Note 10
- Apple iPhone X

## I Recommend:

**Type:** Godefa
**Specs:**
- Lenses Included: Telephoto, Wide Angle, Macro, Kaleidoscope, CPL
- Compatible With iPhone & Samsung Devices
- Tripod Included
- Shutter Remote Included

**Price:** ($25.99)
**Location:** www.amazon.com

### Pro Tips For Shooting Excellent Product photography:

- As you shoot the photos adjust the lighting often until you get your desired results.
- Shoot your product images from several different angles.
- Do not solely use the automatic feature on your camera, which means try to shoot some images by manually setting your (ISO) and shutter speeds.
- If you are new to the art of photography you may want to purchase a book on how to effectively shoot product images and set up a professional studio.

### Software Recommended For Editing Your Product Images:

Another essential aspect to obtaining professional product listing images is editing them post shooting. To effectively edit your product images, I recommend purchasing and learning Adobe Photoshop commonly known simply as Photoshop. Photoshop is a computer software program that comes preloaded with various editing tools that allow the user to render any image, correct any mistakes made when shooting the image, clean an image up by making it clearer, remove unwanted backgrounds, add backgrounds, or add text and graphics to the image. Understanding this software is an essential part of successfully editing your product images.

If you are new to design work in general or via Adobe software programs from a newbie's perspective Photoshop may appear overly technical. Do not be dissuaded by this appearance. With the correct lessons, time, and dedication, Photoshop is fairly easy to purchase, install, download to your computer, learn, master, and use on your own without taking an expensive college style educational course.

**To Purchase, Install, & Download Adobe Photoshop For A $20.99 Monthly Fee For Your Computer, follow the instructional steps included with the labeled images below:**

The downloading and installation process for Adobe Photoshop is similar regardless of whether you are using a **(PC)** or a **(Mac)**.

**Step #1:** Navigate to www.adobe.com from within the Google Chrome Web Browser.

**Step #2:** Using your mouse, left-click and release on the "Sign In" navigational task button located on the top right-hand side of Adobe's homepage:

| Adobe | Creativity & Design | Marketing & Commerce | PDF & E-signatures | Business Solutions | Support | Sign In |

**Step #3:** If you are not a member you will create an Adobe ID. Using your mouse, left-click and release on "Get an Adobe ID." If you are a member you will simply left-click the blue "Sign In" button, sign into your Adobe account, and skip ahead to Step #5:

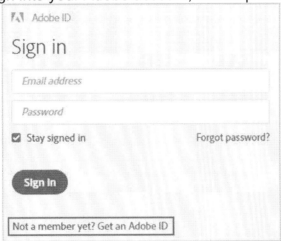

**Step #4:** Enter the required information. Choose a memorable password and be sure to utilize your company's professional Gmail address you created in Chapter 3, Section 3.7. Using your mouse, left-click and release on the "Sign Up" task button when you finish completing the form:

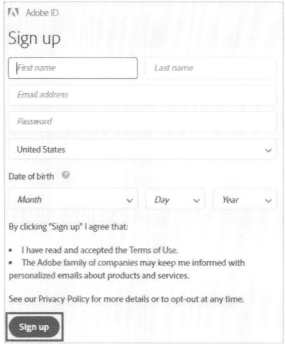

**Step #5:** Using your mouse, left-click and release on the "Creativity & Design" icon located within the taskbar at the top of Adobe's homepage to generate a list of navigational task buttons:

**Step #6:** Using your mouse, left-click and release on the "Photoshop" navigational task button located within the generated list:

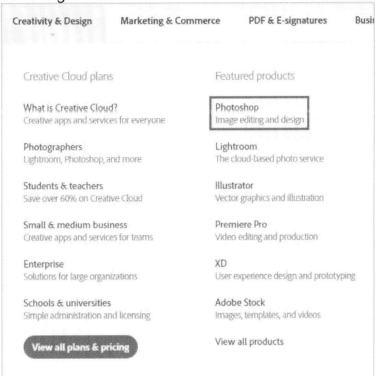

**Step #7:** Using your mouse, left-click and release on the "Buy now" navigational task button located at the top of Adobe Photoshop's homepage:

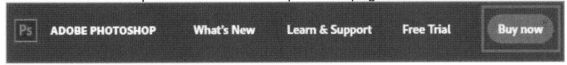

**Step #8:** Using your mouse, left-click and release on the "Buy Now" navigational task button located underneath the section titled Photoshop "Single App":

**Step #9:** Enter the required payment information and then select your preferred monthly or annual subscription type:

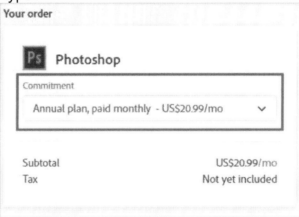

**Step #10:** Using your mouse, left-click and release on the "Place secure order" button to finalize your Photoshop purchase:

**Step #11:** Upon completion of your payment you will be guided to a page that allows you to install and download the software to your (PC) or (Mac). Once Adobe Illustrator is finished installing and downloading you are ready to begin utilizing the software for all your photo editing necessities.

**Step #12:** I recommend pinning (PC) or docking (Mac) the Adobe Photoshop software application launch button to your taskbar or dock for easy daily access as you learned in Chapter 3, Section 3.8:

### To Attain A Comprehensive Training Experience, Build A Strong Design Foundation, And Effectively Learn Adobe Photoshop I Recommend Combining The Following Two Techniques:

**Technique #1:** Watching the tutorials that are provided with the software and simultaneously working along with them in Adobe Photoshop.

### To Locate The Adobe Photoshop Tutorials, follow the instructional steps included with the labeled images below:

**Step #1:** Navigate to www.adobe.com from within the Google Chrome Browser.

**Step #2:** Using your mouse, left-click and release on the "Sign In" navigational task button located on the top right-hand side of Adobe's homepage:

**Step #3:** Enter the required information, then using your mouse, left-click and release on the "Sign In" task button to sign into your Adobe account:

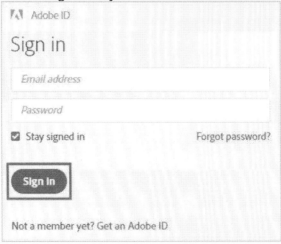

**Step #4:** Using your mouse, left-click and release on the "Creativity & Design" button located within the taskbar at the top of Adobe's homepage to generate a list of navigational task buttons:

**Creativity & Design**

**Step #5:** Using your mouse, left-click and release on the "Photoshop" navigational task button located within the generated list:

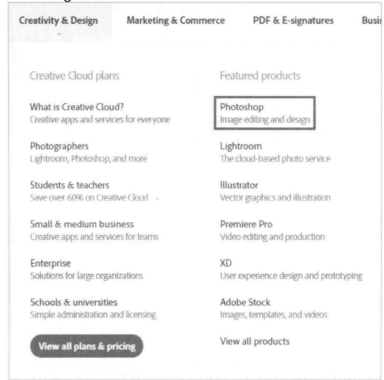

**Step #6:** Using your mouse, left-click and release on the "Learn & Support" navigational task button located within the Adobe Photoshop taskbar at the top of the webpage:

**Step #7:** As you can observe in the screenshot below, you have been navigated to Adobe Photoshop's "Learn & Support" page. This is your access to Photoshop University. It contains tutorials that cover basic, intermediate, and advanced image editing techniques. It explains the how, why, and when to utilize Photoshop's multitude of rendering tools for your artistic needs:

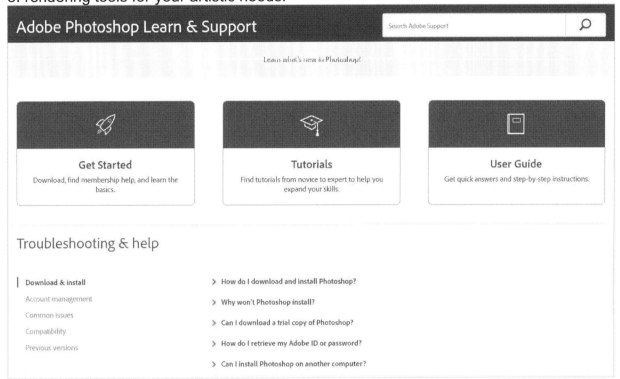

**Technique #2:** Purchasing and working through the step by step (15) lesson plan manual/workbook from Adobe Press:

- Adobe
- Titled: "Adobe Photoshop CC"
- 2019 Release
- Authors: Andrew Faulkner & Conrad Chavez

**Image:** Cover Art For "Photoshop CC" Classroom In A Book

## To Purchase "Adobe Photoshop CC":

*To purchase either a Paperback, e-Book, or Web Edition version navigate to www.adobepress.com from within the Google Chrome Web Browser and locate the book utilizing the provided search bar:

*If you feel that learning Adobe Photoshop and editing your product images is unfeasible or simply not appealing to you, you can choose to outsource your editing work by hiring a professional online.

## To Outsource & Hire A Professional Photo Editor Refer To Any Of The Websites Below From Within The Google Chrome Web Browser:

- Bookmark #17: www.peopleperhour.com
- Bookmark #18: www.upwork.com
- Bookmark #19: www.fiverr.com
- Bookmark #20: www.freelancer.com
- Bookmark #21: www.99designs.com

# Method #2:

## • Outsourcing your product photography:

If you feel that shooting product photography and editing your images with Adobe Photoshop is unfeasible or simply not appealing to you, you can choose to outsource the work entirely by hiring a professional product photography company online.

**To Outsource & Hire A Professional Product Photography Company Refer To Any Of The Websites Below From Within The Google Chrome Web Browser:**

- Bookmark #22: https://ripen.com

**The Process Of Utilizing Ripen For Your Product Photography Needs:**

- Tell Them What You Require & Apply For A Price Quote On Their Website
- Receive A Price Quote
- Ship Your Products To Them
- Communicate With Their Product Photography Team Throughout The Process
- Pay For Their Services
- Receive Your Product Images Digitally Via Email
- They Will Then Ship Your Merchandise Back To You

**What Ripen Offers Their Customers:**

**(9)** Images Total Per Product Listing:

- **(1)** Main Lead Product Image With A White Background
- **(4)** Images Showing Your Products Specs & Features
- **(1)** Lifestyle (Product Use) Image
- **(3)** Images Showing Detail Of The Product With A White Background

*Understanding how to obtain professional high-resolution product images for your Amazon listings is another significant essential milestone to becoming and remaining a successful Amazon Seller.

# To-Do List Chapter 13:

- o Purchase The Required Product Photography Equipment.
- o Purchase, Install, & Download Adobe Photoshop For A $20.99 Monthly Fee For Your Computer.
- o Watch The Photoshop Tutorials Provided By Adobe.
- o Purchase & Work Through "Adobe Photoshop CC-Classroom In A book-The official training workbook from Adobe."
- o Download Any Invoices From Purchasing Photography Equipment & Place Them In Your Microsoft Word Document, Titled, "Amazon Business Invoices," From Section 3.11.
- o Record The Photography Equipment Expenditures Into Your Microsoft Excel Spreadsheet Titled, "Amazon Business Finances," From Section 3.11.
- o Download Your Monthly Invoice For Your $20.99 Adobe Photoshop Subscription & Place It In Your Microsoft Word Document, Titled, "Amazon Business Invoices," From Section 3.11.
- o Record The $20.99 Monthly Adobe Photoshop Subscription Fee Into Your Microsoft Excel Spreadsheet Titled, "Amazon Business Finances," From Section 3.11.
- o Download The Invoice From Purchasing The "Adobe Photoshop CC-Classroom In A Book-The Official training workbook from Adobe" & Place It In Your Microsoft Word Document, Titled, "Amazon Business Invoices," From Section 3.11.
- o Record The Purchase Fee For The "Adobe Photoshop CC-Classroom In A Book-The Official training workbook from Adobe" Into Your Microsoft Excel Spreadsheet Titled, "Amazon Business Finances," From Section 3.11

# Chapter 14:

## Building Professional Product Listings:

As an Amazon Seller it is important to understand that customers shopping on Amazon are doing so through utilization of either the product categories section or more typically the Amazon search bar which relies on the A9 algorithm. Therefore, in order for your listing to effectively be located by customers on Amazon you must choose the correct category to place your merchandise in as well as have the most relevant keywords in relation to your product strategically placed throughout your title, bullet points, description, and backend. The first step in successfully building a product listing relies on conducting the proper keyword research to locate the keywords and keyword phrases that receive the highest per month customer search volume on Amazon for your specific type of merchandise. You will then utilize the most valuable keywords and keyword phrases you discover in your research to create the copy for each aspect of your product listing.

How to conduct proper keyword research, choose what keywords best suit your needs, decide how to optimally utilize those keywords, and elect where to place them in your product listing can be an overwhelming task for some Amazon Sellers new to this process. To alleviate the stressfulness often associated with keyword research and provide you with a comprehensive understanding of the topic I have chosen an example product I designed that I will be using in this chapter's tutorial to walk you through the step-by-step process of how to effectively build a well-optimized product listing. The specific outlined formula I provide you within the following lesson can be utilized for each new product listing you build.

**As You Can Observe In The Image Below, The Product I Will Be Utilizing For The Following Lessons On Keyword Research & Building A Product Listing Is Commonly Known As A "Yoga Mat Bag" Which Is Utilized To Carry As Well As Store A Yoga Mat:**

## Yoga Mat Bag:

**1)** Primary Company Name= "UP"

**2)** Brand Name= "Namaste"

**3)** Color=Black

**4)** Dimensions= Length=(30"), Diameter=(7")

**5)** Material=(100%) Waterproof Canvas Sewn With Reinforced Double Stitching

**6)** Features= Adjustable Strap, (3) Storage Pockets, Ring On One Pocket Can Be Utilized For Storing Keys Or Carrying A Water Bottle, Easy Slide Secure Zipper On One Pocket, & Hidden Smartphone Pocket With Earbuds Slit

**7)** GS1 Licensed (UPC) Code: (1234567891234)

**8)** Amazon Retail Price: ($19.99)

**9)** (1000) Units

**10)** Product Fulfilment Method: (FBA) Only

**11)** Product Weight: (1) Lb.

**12)** Shipping Weight: (1.25) Lb. In Packaging

**13)** (4) Pockets Total

**14)** Target Audience=Product Is Intended For Use By:

- Adults
- Teens
- Unisex

## To Perform Keyword Phrase Research For The "Title" Of Your Product Listing, follow the instructional steps included with the labeled images below:

The title of your product listing should operate in accordance with your primary lead image to introduce your brand name to the customer, briefly explain the type of merchandise you retail in phrase form, specify its key usage, and ultimately draw the customer into your product listing to convert them into a buyer. Furthermore, in order for consumers to be able to locate your product listing when they utilize the Amazon A9 algorithm based search bar you should place the most valuable, relevant, and explanatory keyword phrases in your title. To locate keyword phrases for use in your title I recommend researching (5) of your top competitor's Amazon product listings from within the specific category you are placing your listing in.

**Step #1:** Navigate to www.amazon.com from within the Google Chrome Web Browser and sign into your Amazon buyers account.

**Step #2:** Perform a search for "Yoga Mat Bag" utilizing the Amazon search bar:

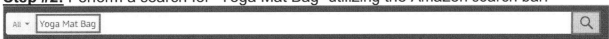

**Step #3:** Locate the first product listing on the page and look for the data provided by Helium 10 which can be located above each product listing. Then, using your mouse, left-click and release on the "Yoga Mat Bags" icon which will navigate you to the Best Sellers product listing page for the specific subcategory that you are currently researching:

> #913 in Sports & Outdoors
> #2 in Yoga Mat Bags
>
> **ASIN:** B07486TF4P  Show
>  Sold by FBA  1 Seller
> Calculate fees

**Image:** Best Sellers Listing Page Icon:

**Step #4:** Once you are navigated to the Best Sellers subcategory product listing page for "Yoga Mat Bags" you will locate (5) of your top selling competitor's product listings that sell similar merchandise to what you will be retailing. The top (5) competitor's you choose should be located within the first (10-20) product listings on the first viewable page within the Amazon Best Sellers list.

**Step #5:** Once you locate the most relevant favorable highest grossing top (5) competitor's you will record each product listings unique (ASIN).

### For Example, Your List Will Resemble:

- (ASIN) B07486TF4P
- (ASIN) B01M2UC0UO
- (ASIN) B01858MWPE
- (ASIN) B005OSMOVA
- (ASIN) B07W6LGR2K

**Step #6:** Navigate to www.helium10.com from within the Google Chrome Web Browser, sign into your account, and be sure to be subscribed to Helium 10's Platinum, Diamond, or Elite membership plan as was discussed in Chapter 4.

**Step #7:** Using your mouse, without clicking, scroll over the Cerebro icon to generate the navigational toolbar:

**Step #8:** Using your mouse, left-click and release on the Cerebro navigational task button to launch the tool:

**Step #9:** Enter the (5) top competitor's (ASINs) from the previous Step #5 into the Helium 10 Cerebro search bar:

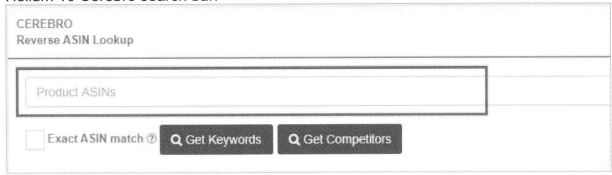

**Step #10:** Using your mouse, left-click and release on the "Get Keywords" task button:

**Step #11:** Using your mouse, left-click and release on the "Advanced Filters" icon to generate a list of filters:

**Step #12:** As you can observe in the image below:

### Title Keyword Phrase Search Formula:

    **1)** Within the section titled "Search Volume" you will place **(1000)** keyword searches per month as the minimum.

    **2)** Within the section titled "Competitor Rank Avg" you will place **(1)** as the minimum and **(48)** as the maximum.

    **3)** Within the section titled "Ranking Competitors" you will place a **(4)** as the minimum.

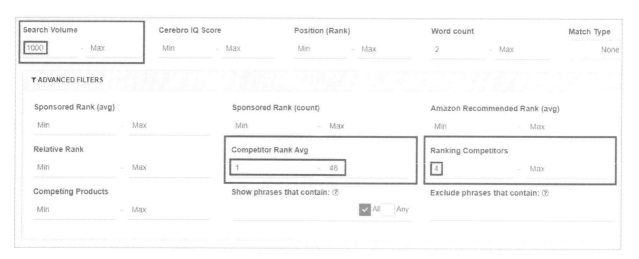

**Step #13:** Using your mouse, left-click and release on the "Apply" button located on the lower right-hand side of the filters section:

**Step #14:** As you can observe in the screenshot below, you have now generated a list containing the (5) most valuable, relevant, and explanatory keyword phrases for "Yoga Mat Bag" that should be utilized for the product listing title:

| # | | Phrase | Cerebro IQ Score | Search Volume | Sponsored ASINs |
|---|---|---|---|---|---|
| | | **Filtered keywords: 5** | | | |
| 1 | ✕ | yoga mat bag ☑ Amazon's Choice | 4,332 | 17,326 | 275 |
| 2 | ✕ | yoga bag ☑ Amazon's Choice | 551 | 11,028 | 251 |
| 3 | ✕ | yoga mat carrier ☑ Amazon's Choice | 4,860 | 4,860 | 274 |
| 4 | ✕ | yoga mat bags and carriers ☑ Amazon's Choice | 1,882 | 1,694 | 270 |
| 5 | ✕ | yoga bags and carriers for women ☑ Amazon's Choice | 1,701 | 1,308 | 0 |

**1)** Yoga mat bag
**2)** Yoga bag
**3)** Yoga mat carrier
**4)** Yoga mat bags and carriers
**5)** Yoga bags and carriers for women

The (5) keyword phrases from the list above contains the primary terms that customers use when they are performing a search on Amazon for a "Yoga Mat Bag" therefore they should be placed within the title of the product listing. If you cannot fit all of the keyword phrases you discover when you utilize this research tactic into the title you can use the remaining terms for the bullet points and description sections of the product listing.

*Note: The title keyword phrase search formula from the above lesson is not specific to "Yoga Mat Bags," which means, depending on the products popularity among customers, you can generally utilize the same formula for all product listing titles you are researching and creating.

**To Perform Keyword Research For The "Bullet Points, Description, & Backend" Of Your Product Listing, follow the instructional steps included with the labeled images below:**

In contrast to the title of an Amazon listing the (5) bullet points will include informative highlights about your product details, specs, and benefits of owning the merchandise being listed. The description will be utilized to showcase your products purpose and functionality in extensive detail to the customer. Furthermore, the description can be used to communicate your brand history, company values, purchase satisfaction guarantee, warranty information when applicable, and brief instructions on proper use if necessary. The backend of your product listing is utilized specifically for (SEO), keyword indexing, and phrase matching purposes. The keywords added to the backend section are not visible to the customer shopping on Amazon.

In order for consumers to be able to locate your product listing when they utilize the Amazon A9 algorithm based search bar each of these sections should contain valuable, relevant, and explanatory keywords. To locate keywords for use in your bullet points, description, and backend I recommend researching (5) of your top competitor's Amazon product listings from within the specific category you are placing your listing in.

**Step #1:** Navigate to www.amazon.com from within the Google Chrome Web Browser and sign into your Amazon buyers account.

**Step #2:** Perform a search for "Yoga Mat Bag" utilizing the Amazon search bar:

**Step #3:** Locate the first product listing on the page and look for the data provided by Helium 10 which can be located above each product listing. Then, using your mouse, left-click and release on the "Yoga Mat Bags" icon which will navigate you to the Best Sellers product listing page for the specific subcategory that you are currently researching:

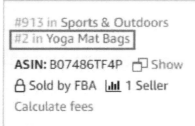

**Image:** Best Sellers Listing Page Icon:

# Amazon Best Sellers
Our most popular products based on sales. Updated hourly.

**Step #4:** Once you are navigated to the Best Sellers subcategory product listing page for "Yoga Mat Bags" you will locate (5) of your top selling competitor's product listings that sell similar merchandise to what you will be retailing. The top (5) competitor's you choose should be located within the first (10-20) product listings on the first viewable page within the Amazon Best Sellers list. As you can observe in the following Step #5, I prefer to utilize the same (ASINs) I located when researching keyword phrases for my product listing title.

**Step #5:** Once you locate the most relevant favorable highest grossing top (5) competitor's you will record each product listings unique (ASIN).

### For Example, Your List Will Resemble:

- (ASIN) B07486TF4P
- (ASIN) B01M2UC0UO
- (ASIN) B01858MWPE
- (ASIN) B005OSMOVA
- (ASIN) B07W6LGR2K

**Step #6:** Navigate to www.helium10.com from within the Google Chrome Web Browser, sign into your account, and be sure to be subscribed to Helium 10's Platinum, Diamond, or Elite membership plan as was discussed in Chapter 4.

**Step #7:** Using your mouse, without clicking, scroll over the Cerebro icon to generate the navigational toolbar:

**Step #8:** Using your mouse, left-click and release on the Cerebro navigational task button to launch the tool:

**Step #9:** Enter the (5) top competitor's (ASINs) from the previous Step #5 into the Helium 10 Cerebro search bar:

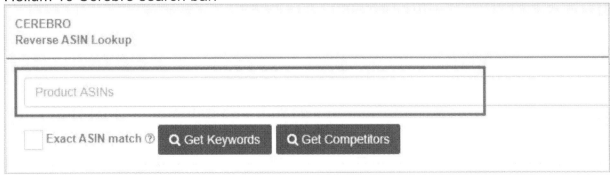

**Step #10:** Using your mouse, left-click and release on the "Get Keywords" task button:

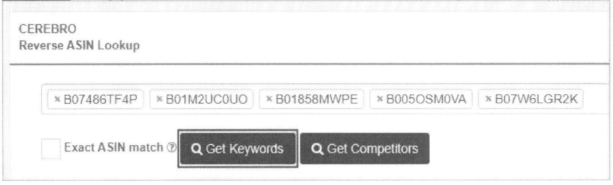

**Step #11:** As you can observe in the image below:

    **1)** Within the section titled "Search Volume" you will place **(1000)** keyword searches per month as the minimum.

*<u>Note:</u> I prefer to place (1000) monthly customer keyword searches per month as the minimum due to the fact that I typically receive the best results on my product listings when utilizing this amount. You could opt to place (500) or (750) within this section if you prefer. Ultimately, the minimum amount is personal preference, but I do not recommend going any lower than (500).

**Step #12:** Using your mouse, left-click and release on the "Apply" button located on the lower right-hand side of the filters section:

**Step #13:** As you can observe in the screenshot below the list now contains (168) keywords and keyword phrases each having a total monthly customer search volume of no less than (1000):

Filtered keywords: 168

**Step #14:** I recommend scrolling through the entire (168) keywords within the list and removing irrelevant keywords and keyword phrases. For example, I would opt to remove the keyword phrase, "Kids Yoga Mat," due to the fact that it has no relevance to my product:

❖ Furthermore, I would remove any keywords and keyword phrases from the list that have another seller's brand name in them, such as "lululemon":

❖ As you can observe in the screenshot below, after completion of step #14 I have decreased the keyword and keyword phrase list down from (168) to a finalized usable total of (51). The list now only contains the most valuable, relevant, and explanatory keywords and keyword phrases in relation to my product:

**Step #15:** You will now export your finalized keyword list from Cerebro into Helium 10's keyword processor Frankenstein. Using your mouse, left-click and release on the "Export" button located on the top right-hand side of the Cerebro page to generate a list of navigational task buttons:

**Step #16:** Using your mouse, left-click and release on the "To Frankenstein" task button to export your keywords and keyword phrases into Frankenstein:

❖ As you can observe in the screenshot below, you have now successfully exported your keywords phrases into the keyword processor Frankenstein:

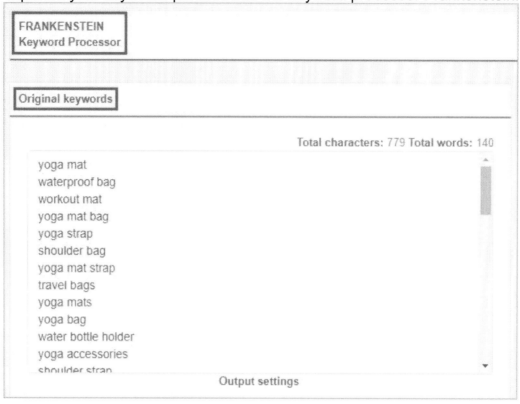

**Step #17:** As you can observe in the screenshot below, when processing your keyword list, I recommend utilizing the following output settings:

- One word/phrase per line
- Remove duplicates
- Convert to lowercase
- Remove common words

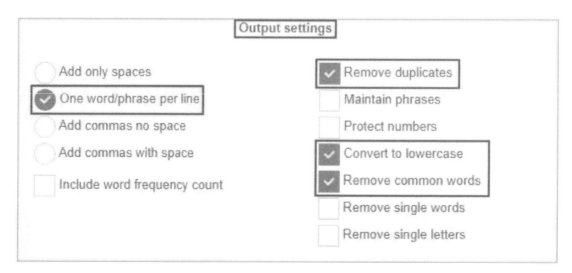

❖ As you can observe in the screenshot below, the output settings have decreased the keyword list to a total of (37). This list contains the keywords that should be utilized to build each aspect of the product listing:

**Step #18:** You will now export your finalized keyword list from Frankenstein into Helium 10's listing optimizer Scribbles to begin building your product listing. Using your mouse, left-click and release on the "Scribbles" task button located on the bottom right-hand side of the Frankenstein page to export your keywords list to Scribbles:

❖ As you can observe in the screenshot below, you have now successfully exported your keywords list into the listing optimizer Scribbles:

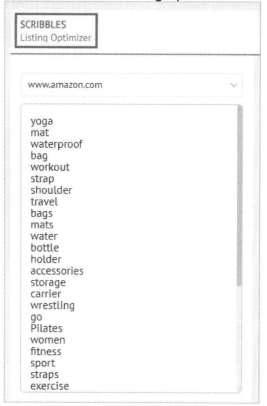

**Step #19:** As you can observe in the screenshot below, you will now manually add the (5) keyword phrases to the keyword list that you researched for your product listing title within the previous tutorial:

  **1)** Yoga mat bag
  **2)** Yoga bag
  **3)** Yoga mat carrier
  **4)** Yoga mat bags and carriers
  **5)** Yoga bags and carriers for women

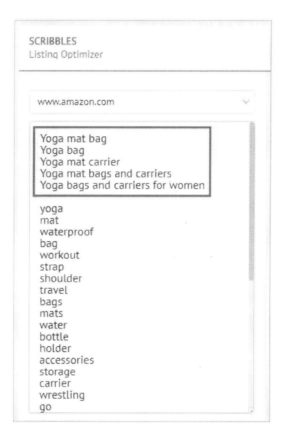

**Step #20:** Using your mouse, left-click and release on the "Apply" task button:

❖ As you can observe in the screenshot below, you have now completed a finalized organized list containing the primary keywords as well as (5) most valuable, relevant, and explanatory keyword phrases for "Yoga Mat Bag" that should be utilized when building the product listing:

**Step #21:** Utilize your keyword phrases within Scribbles to write and build your product listing title:

*<u>Note:</u> As you can observe in the screenshot above, I have added the brand name "Namaste" to the beginning of the product listing title. In order to create brand awareness, I recommend adding your brand name to the beginning of all of your product listing titles.

**Step #22:** Utilize your keywords list within Scribbles to write and build your product listing bullet points:

| Bullet Point #1 | 97/100 bytes, 97 characters, 13 words | Ignore |

AB ab Ab ↰ ↱ 😊 ⎘ Copy

100% washable, secure, sturdy, lightweight, soft canvas yoga bag sewn with reinforced stitching.

| Bullet Point #2 | 90/100 bytes, 90 characters, 16 words | Ignore |

AB ab Ab ↰ ↱ 😊 ⎘ Copy

Dimensions perfectly fit 1/2" or 1/4" thick exercise, pilates, mediation, & yoga mats.

| Bullet Point #3 | 57/100 bytes, 57 characters, 7 words | Ignore |

AB ab Ab ↰ ↱ 😊 ⎘ Copy

Adjustable shoulder strap for customized carrying length.

| Bullet Point #4 | Limit: 100 ⊘ ⊗ |

AB ab Ab ↰ ↱ 😊 ⎘ Copy

Includes hidden smartphone holder on the backside with ear bud slit for on-the-go listening.

| Bullet Point #5 | 95/100 bytes, 95 characters, 16 words | Ignore |

AB ab Ab ↰ ↱ 😊 ⎘ Copy

Expandable roomy front cargo pocket: 10.5" x 6" & exterior ring for hanging your water bottle.

**Step #23:** Utilize your keywords list within Scribbles to write and build your product listing description:

Description

AB ab Ab ↰ ↱ 😊 ⎘ Copy

## Example Description:

At "UP" we only use the highest quality materials to manufacture our products and we sincerely care about our customers satisfaction. Our Namaste yoga mat bags are crafted with your needs in mind. With its full zip feature, it's easy to put your yoga mat in the yoga mat bag to keep it clean, organized, and ready for use. The bag dimensions can hold any Yoga, Pilates, or Meditation mat up to 1/2" thick & 30" wide. The adjustable strap makes it simple, handy, and comfortable to carry to and from your yoga class. The waterproof aspect of its design keeps your yoga mat and belongings dry in the event of rain. The 100% canvas material is machine washable for your convenience. (3) large and expandable roomy pockets are ideal for storing your personal belongings and accessories, such as your keys, tablet, extra clothing, and wallet during and after a Yoga, Pilates, Martial Arts, Spin, or General Workout class.

**Step #24:** Utilize your keywords list within Scribbles to write your product listing backend by adding relevant keywords and keyword phrases:

**\*Note:** As you can observe in the screenshot above, in order for your product listing to be located by Spanish consumers I recommend adding a few relevant Spanish keywords and keyword phrases in the backend search terms of each product listing you create.

❖ As you can observe in the screenshot below, each primary keyword and search term from the finalized organized list for "Yoga Mat Bag" has been crossed off which means that they have all been utilized within the product listing:

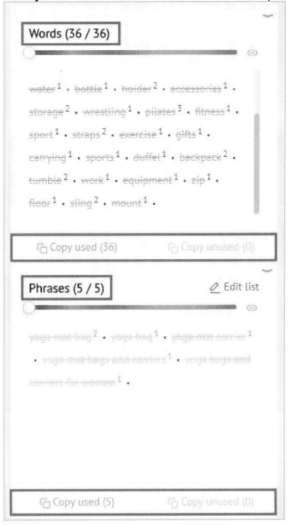

*Note: As you can observe in the screenshot below, there is (5) sections titled "Subject Matter" and numbered (1-5) located on the right-hand side of each bullet point. These sections should be utilized to add any extra relevant, valuable, and explanatory keywords you wish to place into your product listing to trigger Amazon's A9 algorithm when your specific merchandise is searched for by customers on Amazon. Amazon will index up to (50) bytes aka characters worth of keywords for each "Subject Matter" section therefore I highly recommend utilizing these spaces to their maximum potential:

**Step #25:** You will now export your product listing to .TXT so that you can save it on your computer's hard drive. You can then utilize the file to easily copy and paste its contents when you build your product listing within your Amazon Seller Central account. Using your mouse, left-click and release on the "Export" button located on the top right-hand side of the Scribbles page to generate a list of navigational task buttons:

**Step #26:** Using your mouse, left-click and release on the "Export to .TXT" task button:

**Step #27:** Save the .TXT file to your computer's hard drive utilizing a memorable title, such as "(Scribbles)-Yoga Mat Bag."

**To Build A Product Listing, follow the instructional steps included with the labeled images below:**

**Step #1:** Navigate to http://sellercentral.amazon.com from within the Google Chrome Web Browser and sign into your Amazon Seller Central account.

**Step #2:** Using your mouse, without clicking, scroll over the "Catalog" icon located within the taskbar at the top of the Amazon Seller Central dashboard to generate a list of navigational task buttons:

**Step #3:** Using your mouse, left-click and release on the "Add Products" navigational task button located within the generated list:

**Step #4:** Using your mouse left-click and release on the "Create a new product listing" navigational task button:

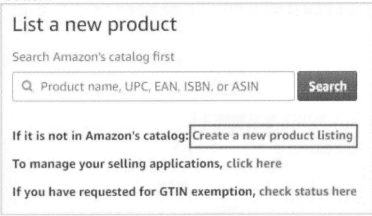

**Step #5:** You will now choose the product category and subcategory to place your product listing within. Using your mouse, left-click and release on the "Sports & Outdoors" navigational task button:

**Step #6:** Using your mouse, left-click and release on the "Sports & Fitness" navigational task button:

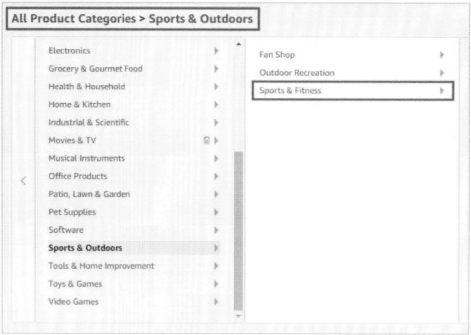

**Step #7:** Using your mouse, left-click and release on the "Yoga" navigational task button:

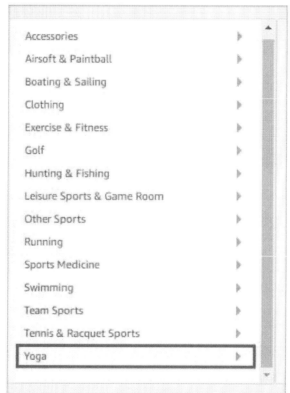

**Step #8:** Using your mouse, left-click and release on the "Mat Bags" navigational task button:

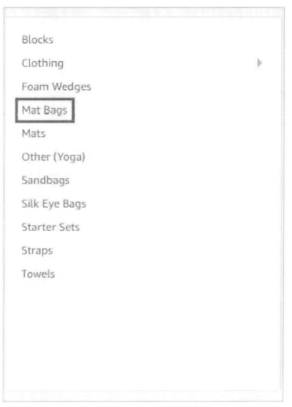

**Step #9:** Using your mouse, left-click and release on the "Select" button located underneath the "Mat Bags" icon to finalize your product listing subcategory selection:

**Step #10:** Using your mouse, left-click and release on the "Advanced View" icon to open all options available for building your product listings:

**Step #11:** Enter your unique licensed GS1 (UPC) code as was discussed in Chapter 9, Section 9.6:

**Step #12:** Using your mouse, left-click and release on the "Select" button to generate a list of options:

| * Product ID ❶ | 1234567891 | - Select - ⬍ |
|---|---|---|

**Step #13:** Using your mouse, left-click and release on the "UPC" icon:

- Select - ⬍
- Select -
GTIN
EAN
ISBN
GCID
UPC
ASIN

**Step #14:** Copy and paste the product listing title from the file titled "(Scribbles)-Yoga Mat Bag" that you created in the previous tutorial utilizing Helium 10's keyword listing optimizer Scribbles:

| Product Name ❶ | Namaste Waterproof Fitness Travel Yoga Mat Bag/Yoga Mat Carrier With (3) Multi-F |
|---|---|

**Step #15:** Enter your primary company name, such as "UP" as was discussed and created in Chapter 5:

| Manufacturer | UP |
|---|---|

**Step #16:** Enter your trademarked brand name as was discussed and created in Chapter 9, Section 9.6:

| Brand Name ❶ | Namaste |
|---|---|

**Step #17:** Enter the primary color of the product:

| Color ❶ | Black |
|---|---|

**Step #18:** Enter the dimensions of the product:

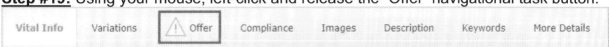

**Step #19:** Using your mouse, left-click and release the "Offer" navigational task button:

**Step #20:** Enter the price of your product will retail for on Amazon:

**Step #21:** Using your mouse, left-click and release on the "Select" button to generate a list of conditions to select from:

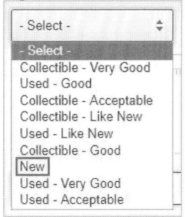

**Step #22:** Select "New" from the generated list of conditions:

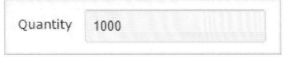

**Step #23:** Enter the initial quantity you will have available for purchase:

**Step #24:** As you can observe in the screenshot below:

(FBM) aka (MFN)="I will ship this item myself"
(FBA)="Amazon will ship and provide customer service"

❖ For this tutorial, the product fulfilment method is (FBA) therefore you will choose the option titled "Amazon will ship and provide customer service":

**Step #25:** Using your mouse, left-click and release on the "Images" navigational task button:

| Vital Info | Variations | Offer | Compliance | Images | Description | Keywords | More Details |

**Step #26:** You will now upload your professional grade high-resolution primary lead product listing image as was discussed in Chapter 13:

**Step #27:** You will now upload (8) additional professional grade high-resolution product listing images as was discussed in Chapter 13

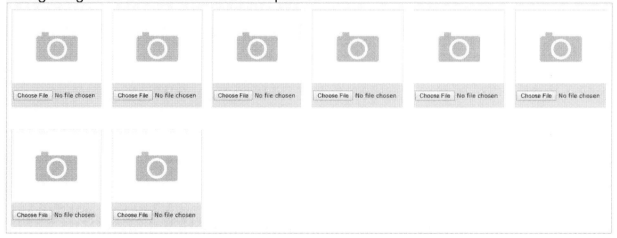

**Step #28:** Using your mouse, left-click and release on the "Description" navigational task button:

| Vital Info | Variations | Offer | Compliance | Images | Description | Keywords | More Details |
|---|---|---|---|---|---|---|---|

**Step #29:** Copy and paste the product listing description from the file titled "(Scribbles)-Yoga Mat Bag" that you created in the previous tutorial utilizing Helium 10's keyword listing optimizer Scribbles:

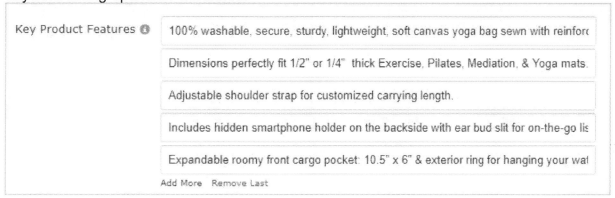

**Step #30:** Copy and paste the product listing bullet points from the file titled "(Scribbles)-Yoga Mat Bag" that you created in the previous tutorial utilizing Helium 10's keyword listing optimizer Scribbles:

Key Product Features

- 100% washable, secure, sturdy, lightweight, soft canvas yoga bag sewn with reinforc
- Dimensions perfectly fit 1/2" or 1/4" thick Exercise, Pilates, Mediation, & Yoga mats.
- Adjustable shoulder strap for customized carrying length.
- Includes hidden smartphone holder on the backside with ear bud slit for on-the-go lis
- Expandable roomy front cargo pocket: 10.5" x 6" & exterior ring for hanging your wat

Add More   Remove Last

**Step #31:** Using your mouse, left-click and release on the "Keywords" navigational task button:

| Vital Info | Variations | Offer | Compliance | Images | Description | Keywords | More Details |
|---|---|---|---|---|---|---|---|

**Step #32:** Utilize the (5) provided sections to add relevant, valuable, and explanatory keywords that state your products intended use:

| Intended Use ⓘ | Yoga Mat Storage |
| --- | --- |
| | Yoga Mat Bag |
| | Yoga Mat Carrier |
| | Yoga Mat Holder |
| | Travel |

Add More   Remove Last

**Step #33:** Enter your specific target audiences:

| Target Audience ⓘ | Adults |
| --- | --- |
| | Teens |
| | Unisex |

Add More   Remove Last

**Step #34:** Enter specific attributes you want your product listing to index for, such as "Waterproof":

| Other Attributes ⓘ | Waterproof |
| --- | --- |

**Step #35:** Copy and paste the product listing subject matter from the file titled "(Scribbles)-Yoga Mat Bag" that you created in the previous tutorial utilizing Helium 10's keyword listing optimizer Scribbles:

| Subject Matter ⓘ | Straps, Sling, Holster, Workout, Tumble, Backpack |
| --- | --- |

Add More   Remove Last

***Note:** If you were truly building a product listing I would recommend utilizing the (4) additional "Subject Matter" sections to add any extra relevant, valuable, and explanatory keywords to trigger Amazon's A9 algorithm when your specific merchandise is searched for by customers on Amazon.

**Step #36:** Copy and paste the product listing backend search terms from the file titled "(Scribbles)-Yoga Mat Bag" that you created in the previous tutorial utilizing Helium 10's keyword listing optimizer Scribbles:

Search Terms ⓘ | yoga mat bags and carriers gifts duffel equipment yoga bags and carriers for women

**Step #37:** Using your mouse, left-click and release on the "More Details" navigational task button:

Vital Info | Variations | Offer | Compliance | Images | Description | Keywords | **More Details**

**Step #38:** Enter your products total shipping weight with individual product and shipping packaging included:

Shipping Weight ⓘ | 1.25 | LB ⇕

**Step #39:** Enter your products total weight without individual product and shipping packaging included:

Weight | 1 | LB ⇕

**Step #40:** Enter your products fabric type:

Fabric Type ⓘ | 100% Canvas

**Step #41:** Enter the number of pockets the product has:

number_of_pockets | 4

**Step #42:** Enter the specific use of the product:

Specific Uses For Product | Yoga Mat Storage

**Step #43:** Enter the products dimensions:

Item Dimensions | Length | Width | Height | |
| --- | --- | --- | --- | --- |
| | | | 30 | IN ⇕ |

**Step #44:** Enter the products diameter:

**Step #45:** If you were truly building a product listing and retailing the "Yoga Mat Bag" you would now "Save and finish" the product listing creation process:

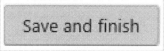

**Pro Tip:**

- For each product listing you create, in order to be certain your product listing is and remains well-optimized, I recommend routinely using Helium 10's software tools Index Checker and Keyword Tracker. Furthermore, to aid you in hijacker and sniper prevention I suggest monitoring your product listing's status through utilization of Helium 10's software tool Alerts as was discussed in Chapter 4.

*Understanding how to build highly optimized professional product listings is another significant essential milestone to becoming and remaining a successful Amazon Seller.

# Chapter 15:

## Determining Your Product Listing Price Points:

There are several factors that will create a basis for determining your Amazon product listing price points, including your overall production costs, your projected (ROI), and your top (5-10) competitor's price range.

### Calculating Production Costs:

To set a product listing price point you must begin by calculating your production costs which you will utilize to determine your projected (ROI).

### When Determining Your Product Listing Price Point Many Important Production Costs Must Be Considered, Such As:

- Manufacturing
- Branding
- Brand Trademark Fees
- Individual Packaging
- (UPC)
- (FNSKU) Labels
- Shipping From Your Supplier To Your Location
- Shipping To The Amazon Fulfillment Center (FBA Only)
- (FBA) Fees (Storage, Pick, Pack, & Shipping) (FBA Only)
- Amazon Referral Fees
- Shipping To The Customer (MFN Only)
- Advertising (Amazon Sponsored Ad Campaigns; Automatic & Manual)
- Amazon's (ERP) Early Reviewer Program; ($60)
- Any & All Costs You Incur Associated With Manufacturing, Packaging, Branding, Labeling, Storing, Shipping, & Marketing The Product

### Determining Your Projected (ROI):

Depending on your overall production costs and the current market price trend for your specific type of merchandise on Amazon I recommend shooting for rate of (100%) (ROI) and no lower than (50%) (ROI) as was discussed in Chapter 8.

### Pricing Your Product Based On That Of Your Top Competitor's Price Range:

Depending on your overall production costs and projected (ROI) I recommend initially pricing your merchandise a bit lower than that of your top competitors. Competitively pricing your merchandise will assist you in obtaining initial sales and customer reviews. Once you create brand awareness, your product listing gains traction, and you begin to rise in page rank ultimately creating a footprint on Amazon within the specific category you are retailing I then recommend raising your product listing price point to match that of your competitors.

*Note: Some Amazon Sellers opt to retail their merchandise for higher than market value in comparison to that of their competitors. I only recommend utilizing this tactic if your product is truly superior in some manner that would constitute a higher price point to that of your competitors, such as the item having an added feature, being comprised of better quality materials, or retailing with an accompanied item.

*Understanding how to determine your product listing price points is another significant essential milestone to becoming and remaining a successful Amazon Seller.

# Chapter 16:

# Product Launch Marketing Campaign, Amazon (PPC) Sponsored Ads, Lightning Deals, (7) Day Deals, & Determining (ACOS):

Once your product listing is created, you have set your product price point, and you are officially selling your merchandise on Amazon it will be time to conduct your product launch marketing campaign. Your campaign should entail a combination of generating a digital promotional discount coupon on Amazon as well as running (1) Automatic and (1) Manual (PPC) Sponsored Ad. Your product launch will assist you in obtaining initial sales, customer reviews, and help your product listing appear on the first page an Amazon customer views when they utilize your specific keywords and keyword phrases to search for your merchandise. Once you create brand awareness, your product listing gains traction, you create a footprint on Amazon within the specific category you are retailing, and you begin to observe organic sales you can then typically decrease expenditures associated with coupon generation and (PPC) Sponsored Ad campaigns.

**To Generate A Digital Promotional Discount Coupon For Your Product Listing On Amazon, follow the instructional steps included with the labeled images below:**

When you generate a coupon for your listing it will be discoverable by customers on Amazon through several means:

- Amazon's Coupons Home Page
- Customer Search Results
- Product Detail Pages
- On Your Offer Listings Page
- In Their Carts At Checkout

**Step #1:** Navigate to http://sellercentral.amazon.com from within the Google Chrome Web Browser and sign into your Amazon Seller Central account.

**Step #2:** Using your mouse, without clicking, scroll over the "Advertising" icon located within the taskbar at the top of the Amazon Seller Central dashboard to generate a list of navigational task buttons:

**Step #3:** Using your mouse, left-click and release on the "Coupons" navigational task button located within the generated list:

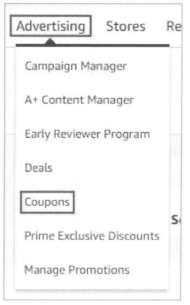

**Step #4:** Using your mouse, left-click and release on the "Create your first coupon" navigational task button located on the top right-hand side of the Seller Central coupons page:

**Step #5:** Enter your product listing (ASIN) into the provided section:

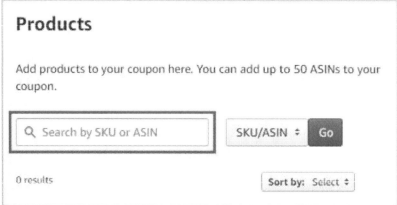

**Step #6:** Using your mouse, left-click and release on the "Go" task button:

**Step #7:** Using your mouse, left-click and release on the "Add to coupon" task button:

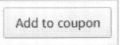

**Step #8:** Using your mouse, left-click and release on the "Continue to next step" navigational task button located on the top right-hand side of the coupons page:

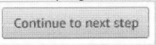

**Step #9:** Choose whether you prefer to have your coupon state money or percentage off of the retail price:

- % Must Be A Rate Between **(5-80%)** Off Of The Retail Price
- $ Must Be A Rate Of **($1)** Or More

*<u>Note:</u> In order to receive a large volume of sales in a brief period of time and ultimately help your product listing rank faster to the top of page one I recommend creating a coupon that has a discount rate of at least (25%) off. Essentially, customers will be much more apt to impulsively purchase a product with a (25%) discount in comparison to a product with, per say, a (10%) discount. Furthermore, if you wish to speed up the sales receival process you could opt to create a (50%) discount coupon code. The higher the percentage of discount you offer within your coupons the quicker you will sell your allotted promotional stock.

**Step #10:** You will enter either the discount dollar or percentage amount you have designated for your coupon:

**Step #11:** To prevent retail arbitragers from purchasing your entire allotted discounted stock utilizing all of your coupons in one purchase and reselling your merchandise for a higher price directly on your product listing, Amazon, or alternative marketplaces, I recommend only allowing one coupon redemption per customer. To do so, using your mouse, left-click and release on the section titled "Yes, limit redemption to one per customer":

Do you want to limit the redemption of your coupon to 1 per customer?

⦿ Yes, limit redemption to one per customer

◯ No, allow my coupon to be redeemed multiple times by same customer

**Step #12:** You will now set your total allotted coupon budget:

## Budget

$ [                    ]

$100.00 minimum

### How Allotted Coupon Budgets Operate:

- Amazon charges you ($.60) for each coupon that is redeemed.
- Your coupons are taken offline when you reach (80%) of your total allotted budget.

### For example, per say, you sell:

A "Yoga Mat Bag" for ($19.99).

### You create a coupon that offers a (25%) discount:

($19.99 x .25=$4.99)

*Each coupon will equal a rate of ($4.99) towards your total allotted coupon budget.

### You set your coupon budget at $500:

($500 x .80=$400)
(80% of $500=$400)

\*That means that your total allotted coupon budget is truly ($400). When your budget reaches ($400) your coupon will no longer be active and will be taken offline.

**Total amount of coupons an allotted budget of ($400) will generate:**

(71 Coupons x $4.99= $354.29)
(71 Coupons x $.60 Amazon Redemption Fee=$42.60)
($354.29 + $42.60=$396.29)

\*That means that an allotted budget of ($400) will generate a total of approximately (71) coupons.

\***Note:** In order to observe positive results from your product launch I recommend generating no less than (100) coupons at a rate of (25%) off your product listing retail price.

**Pro Tip:**

To account for a portion of your losses from offering discounted coupons you could opt to initially price your overall product listing higher during your product launch than what you will normally retail your merchandise for. For example, per say, you will typically sell a "Yoga Mat Bag" at a rate of ($19.99). During your product launch and coupon generating phase you could instead opt to initially retail the item at a rate of ($21.99) to cover a portion of the discounted coupon price. You could then drop your product listing price back down to ($19.99) after your coupons have all been utilized, are no longer active, and have been taken offline.

**Step #13:** Using your mouse, left-click and release on the "Continue to next step" navigational task button located on the top right-hand side of the coupons page:

Continue to next step

**Step #14:** You will now create and add an enticing title to your coupon:

**Coupon title** (what customers will see)

For a more effective coupon title, choose a definition that accurately describes the product group you added to your coupon. Example: "Save 15% on hand sanitizers"

| Save 25% on | | Title Guidelines |

**Step #15:** You will now set the schedule for when you prefer to have your promotional coupon available for use by customers on Amazon and what date you wish it to become inactive if you have not reached your allotted coupon budget. During your product launch I recommend running a discounted coupon for no less than (30) days starting from the day you first list your product on Amazon.

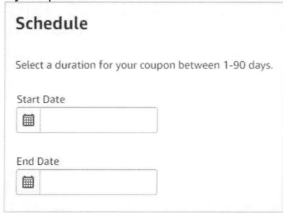

**Step #16:** Using your mouse, left-click and release on the "Continue to next step" navigational task button located on the top right-hand side of the coupons page:

**Step #17:** I recommend reviewing your coupon data to make sure it has been correctly entered. Once you are finished revising your coupon you will submit it. To do so, using your mouse, left-click and release on the "Submit coupon" to complete the process:

**\*Note:** Depending on the health of your product listing sales volume you can opt to run post product launch coupons at any time you deem necessary to assist you in obtaining a higher conversion velocity. I typically prefer to produce (100) coupons (4) months postdate of my product launch. Furthermore, generating promotional discount coupons during the months of November and December is an exceptional marketing technique to utilize to help you acquire sales during the competitive holiday season.

## <u>To Monitor The Performance, Success, Start Date, & End Date Of Your</u> <u>Promotional Coupons, follow the instructional steps included with the labeled</u> <u>images below:</u>

**Step #1:** Navigate to http://sellercentral.amazon.com from within the Google Chrome Web Browser and sign into your Amazon Seller Central account.

**Step #2:** Using your mouse, without clicking, scroll over the "Advertising" icon located within the taskbar at the top of the Amazon Seller Central dashboard to generate a list of navigational task buttons:

**Step #3:** Using your mouse, left-click and release on the "Manage Promotions" navigational task button located within the generated list:

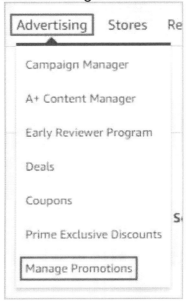

❖ As you can observe in the screenshot below, you have now been navigated to the promotion's manager:

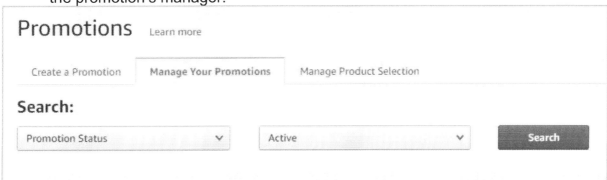

## To Create An Automatic (PPC) Sponsored Ad Campaign, follow the instructional steps included with the labeled images below:

When you create an Automatic (PPC) Sponsored Ad campaign Amazon's A9 algorithm will instinctively utilize a combination of the type of product you sell, the category/subcategory your product resides in, the keywords you utilized to write your product listing, and your competitor's product listing information to specifically target and advertise your goods to buyers searching for the type of merchandise you retail. Ultimately, when Amazon customers are searching for merchandise using the specific keywords and keyword phrases associated with the merchandise you retail then your Sponsored Ad will automatically display in their search results. These ads will help your brand become visible on Amazon, create sales volume, and ultimately assist you in ranking to page one of customer search results.

Although there are costs associated with running (PPC) Sponsored Ads, depending on your financial situation, I recommend making it a regular practice to set aside an allotted budget to create (1) Automatic campaign for each product listing you build. I then suggest letting it run on Amazon for a term of no less than (30) days. Once the campaign produces results you can then examine the statistical data it generates to confirm whether the cost of the Sponsored Ad is worth the expenditure or not. In some cases, after (30) days you may need to adjust specific features of the campaign, such as adding negative keywords and negative keyword phrases to suit your exact advertising agenda by better targeting your intended audience. Furthermore, the information obtained from Automatic Sponsored Ad campaign reports can be utilized to optimize your Manual Sponsored Ad campaigns by informing you of particular valuable keywords and keyword phrases you may not have located when you performed the initial keyword research for your product listing. You can then opt to individually add your findings to your Manual (PPC) Sponsored Ad Campaign.

**Step #1:** Navigate to http://sellercentral.amazon.com from within the Google Chrome Web Browser and sign into your Amazon Seller Central account.

**Step #2:** Using your mouse, without clicking, scroll over the "Advertising" icon located within the taskbar at the top of the Amazon Seller Central dashboard to generate a list of navigational task buttons:

**Step #3:** Using your mouse, left-click and release on the "Campaign Manager" navigational task button located within the generated list:

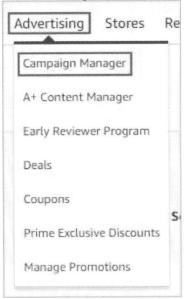

**Step #4:** Using your mouse, left-click and release on the "Continue" navigational task button located within the section titled "Sponsored Products":

**Step #5:** You will now name your campaign. For organizational purposes, I recommend choosing a title that is memorable and represents the exact product you retail:

**Step #6:** Set a "Start" and "End" date for the term of your campaign. As I previously stated, in order to observe the effectiveness of the campaign and to produce examinable statistical data results I recommend allowing the Automatic Sponsored Ads to initially run for a term of no less than (30) days:

**Step #7:** Set a daily budget. If your financial situation allows for the expense I recommend starting with a daily budget of no less than ($10), which ultimately means you could incur a cost of up to ($300) a month ad spend for this particular marketing campaign. Please be aware, that you can always adjust your daily budget amount at any time you deem necessary to better suit your exact advertising needs. In some cases, ($10) a day is simply operates solely as a preliminary starting amount to assist you in producing examinable statistical data results. Ultimately, depending on the competitiveness of the product you retail, your daily budget may require modifications to truly be effective, produce desirable results, and generate substantial sales volume:

**Step #8:** You will now choose "Automatic targeting" to designate the type of Sponsored Ad you are creating, which is an Automatic Campaign:

**Step #9:** Although there are other options available, when initially running an Automatic Sponsored Ad campaign, until you generate examinable results, I recommend utilizing the "Dynamic bids- down only" option for your keyword bidding strategy. Please be aware, that you can always adjust your bidding strategy at any time you deem necessary to better suit your exact advertising needs.

*Alternatively, you could opt to utilize the "Dynamic Bids" setting for the first (2) weeks of your initial Automatic Sponsored Ad campaign and then modify your campaign to run on the "Dynamic Bids- Up and Down" setting for the remaining (2) weeks. You can then compare and contrast the statistical data results each setting produces to determine the efficiency of each strategy and then run your next Automatic Sponsored Ad Campaign solely utilizing the most effective method. Ultimately, depending on the competitiveness of the product you retail, your bidding strategy may require adjustment to truly be effective, produce desirable results, and generate substantial sales volume:

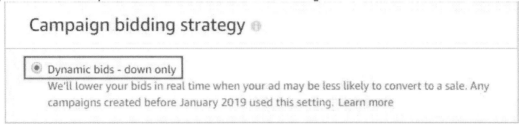

**Step #10:** You will now title your "Ad group name." For organizational purposes, I recommend choosing a title that is memorable and represents the exact product category/subcategory you are retailing within:

**Step #11:** You will now add the (ASIN) of the product listing you are promoting for this campaign:

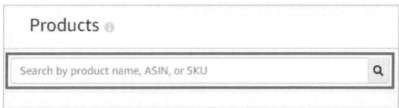

**Step #12:** Set your preferred (PPC) bid. This value represents the highest monetary amount you are willing to pay per customer click for your Automatic Sponsored Ad. When initially running an Automatic Sponsored Ad campaign, until you generate examinable results, I recommend setting your (PPC) bid at ($.50). A (PPC) bid of ($.50) on an ad budget of ($10) a day allows you the ability to receive at least approximately (20) customer clicks per day when your keywords or keyword phrases are utilized to display your Automatic Sponsored Ad. Please be aware, that you can always adjust your (PPC) bid amount up or down at any time you deem necessary to better suit your exact advertising needs.

*Alternatively, you could opt to set your (PPC) bid at ($.50) for the first week of your initial Automatic Sponsored Ad campaign and then modify your (PPC) bid amount by gradually raising it each week by, per say, a rate of ($.25) for the remainder of the month. You can then compare and contrast the statistical data results each (PPC) bid alteration produces to determine the efficiency of each amount and then run your next Automatic Sponsored Ad Campaign solely utilizing the most effective pricing method. Ultimately, depending on the competitiveness of the product you retail, your (PPC) bid amounts may require monetary adjustments to truly be effective, produce desirable results, and generate substantial sales volume:

**Step #13:** Using your mouse, left-click and release on the "Launch campaign" task button to finish creating your Automatic (PPC) Sponsored Ad and officially make the campaign active on Amazon:

Launch campaign

**To Create A Manual (PPC) Sponsored Ad Campaign, follow the instructional steps included with the labeled images below:**

When you create a Manual (PPC) Sponsored Ad "Keyword Targeting" campaign you will select specific keywords and keyword phrases that you deem relevant to the associated merchandise you retail. Then Amazon's A9 algorithm will utilize your designated keywords to specifically target and advertise your product listing to buyers searching for the type of product you sell. Ultimately, when Amazon customers are searching for merchandise using the specific keywords and keyword phrases you add to your campaign then your Sponsored Ad will display in their search results. Alternatively, you can opt to create a Manual (PPC) Sponsored Ad "Product Targeting" campaign that solely targets consumers through utilization of a combination of the type of product you sell, the category/subcategory your product resides in, your brand name, and your product features. If you select the latter option, Amazon's A9 algorithm will utilize your designated product type, category/subcategory, brand name, and product features to specifically target and advertise your product listing to buyers based on your designated product listing attributes. Both of these Manual (PPC) Sponsored Ad types will help your brand become visible on Amazon, create sales volume, and ultimately assist you in ranking to page one of customer search results.

Although there are costs associated with running (PPC) Sponsored Ads, depending on your financial situation, I recommend making it a regular practice to set aside an allotted budget to create (1) Manual campaign for each product listing you build. I then suggest letting it run on Amazon for a term of no less than (30) days. Once the campaign produces results you can then examine the statistical data it generates to confirm whether the cost of the Sponsored Ad is worth the expenditure or not. In some cases, after (30) days you may need to adjust specific features of the campaign, such as adding negative keywords or altering the keywords and keyword phrases you initially selected to suit your exact advertising agenda by better targeting your intended audience.

**Step #1:** Navigate to http://sellercentral.amazon.com from within the Google Chrome Web Browser and sign into your Amazon Seller Central account.

**Step #2:** Using your mouse, without clicking, scroll over the "Advertising" icon located within the taskbar at the top of the Amazon Seller Central dashboard to generate a list of navigational task buttons:

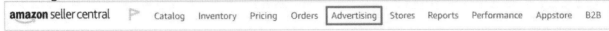

**Step #3:** Using your mouse, left-click and release on the "Campaign Manager" navigational task button located within the generated list:

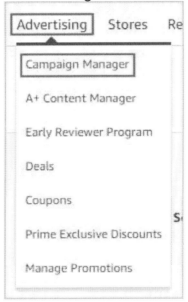

**Step #4:** Using your mouse, left-click and release on the "Continue" navigational task button located within the section titled "Sponsored Products":

**Step #5:** You will now name your campaign. For organizational purposes, I recommend choosing a title that is memorable and represents the exact product you retail:

**Step #6:** Set a "Start" and "End" date for the term of your campaign. As I previously stated, in order to observe the effectiveness of the campaign and to produce examinable statistical data results I recommend allowing the Manual Sponsored Ads to initially run for a term of no less than (30) days:

**Step #7:** Set a daily budget. If your financial situation allows for the expense I recommend starting with a daily budget of no less than ($10), which ultimately means you could incur a cost of up to ($300) a month ad spend for this particular marketing campaign. Please be aware, that you can always adjust your daily budget amount at any time you deem necessary to better suit your exact advertising needs. In some cases, ($10) a day is simply operates solely as a preliminary starting amount to assist you in producing examinable statistical data results. Ultimately, depending on the competitiveness of the product you retail, your daily budget may require modifications to truly be effective, produce desirable results, and generate substantial sales volume:

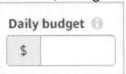

**Step #8:** You will now choose "Manual targeting" to designate the type of Sponsored Ad you are creating, which is a Manual Campaign:

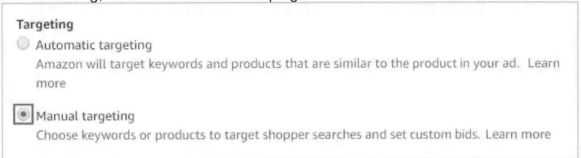

**Step #9:** Although there are other options available, when initially running a Manual Sponsored Ad campaign, until you generate examinable results, I recommend utilizing the "Dynamic bids- down only" option for your keyword bidding strategy. Please be aware, that you can always adjust your bidding strategy at any time you deem necessary to better suit your exact advertising needs.

   *Alternatively, you could opt to utilize the "Dynamic Bids" setting for the first (2) weeks of your initial Manual Sponsored Ad campaign and then modify your campaign to run on the "Dynamic Bids- Up and Down" setting for the remaining (2) weeks. You can then compare and contrast the statistical data results each setting produces to determine the efficiency of each strategy and then run your next Manual Sponsored Ad Campaign solely utilizing the most effective method. Ultimately, depending on the competitiveness of the product you retail, your bidding strategy may require adjustment to truly be effective, produce desirable results, and generate substantial sales volume:

**Step #10:** You will now title your "Ad group name." For organizational purposes, I recommend choosing a title that is memorable and represents the exact product category/subcategory you are retailing within:

**Step #11:** You will now add the (ASIN) of the product listing you are promoting for this campaign:

Products ⊙

| Search by product name, ASIN, or SKU | 🔍 |

**Step #12:** For this campaign type I will be teaching you how to manually select and enter specific keyword phrases that are relevant to an associated type of merchandise, therefore you will choose the "Keyword targeting" option. For each product listing you create I recommend running (1) Manual (PPC) Sponsored Ad campaign that specifically targets keywords and keyword phrases that customers utilize to search for the type of merchandise you retail. Then, depending on your financial situation, you could opt to run a separate Manual (PPC) Sponsored Ad campaign by utilizing the "Product targeting" setting:

Targeting ⊙

You can add multiple ad groups to your campaign, but you can choose only one targeting type per ad group.

◉ Keyword targeting
   Choose keywords to help your products appear in shopper searches. Learn more

Use this strategy when you know the search terms that customers use to search products similar to yours.

**Step #13:** Using your mouse, left-click and release on the "Enter list" task button:

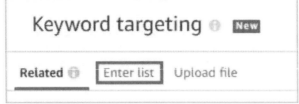

**Step #14:** Set your preferred (PPC) bid. This value represents the highest monetary amount you are willing to pay per customer click for your Manual Sponsored Ad. When initially running a Manual Sponsored Ad campaign, until you generate examinable results, I recommend setting your (PPC) bid at ($.50). A (PPC) bid of ($.50) on an ad budget of ($10) a day allows you the ability to receive at least approximately (20) customer clicks per day when your targeted keywords or keyword phrases are utilized to display your Manual Sponsored Ad. Please be aware, that you can always adjust your (PPC) bid amount up or down at any time you deem necessary to better suit your exact advertising needs.

      *Alternatively, you could opt to set your (PPC) bid at ($.50) for the first week of your initial Manual Sponsored Ad campaign and then modify your (PPC) bid amount by gradually raising it each week by, per say, a rate of ($.25) for the remainder of the month. You can then compare and contrast the statistical data results each (PPC) bid alteration produces to determine the efficiency of each amount and then run your next Manual Sponsored Ad Campaign solely utilizing the most effective pricing method. Ultimately, depending on the competitiveness of the product you retail, your (PPC) bid amounts may require monetary adjustments to truly be effective, produce desirable results, and generate substantial sales volume:

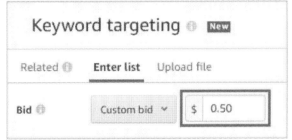

**Step #15:** Select your preferred match type. Although there are other options available, when initially running a Manual Sponsored Ad campaign, until you generate examinable results, I recommend utilizing all (3) match types. Please be aware, that you can always adjust your match types at any time you deem necessary to better suit your exact advertising needs.

*Alternatively, you could test each match type by opting to utilize all (3) match types for the first week you run your campaign and then successively modifying your strategy on a weekly basis by solely utilizing Broad for (1) week, Phrase for (1) week, and Exact for (1) week. You can then compare and contrast the statistical data results each match type setting produces to determine the efficiency of each strategy and then run your next Manual Sponsored Ad Campaign solely utilizing the most effective method. Ultimately, depending on the competitiveness of the product you retail, the match type you designate for your campaign may require adjustment to truly be effective, produce desirable results, and generate substantial sales volume:

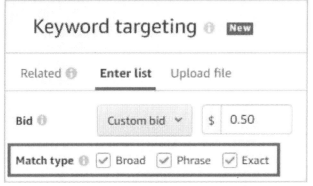

If you choose to test each match type setting to locate the most effective option your Manual (PPC) Sponsored Ad campaign schedule will resemble:

- Week (1): Broad, Phrase, Exact
- Week (2): Broad
- Week (3): Phrase
- Week (4): Exact

**Step #16:** Enter the specific keywords and keyword phrases for the audience you intend on targeting.

*For "Keyword Targeting" purposes, I recommend utilizing the (5) most valuable, relevant, and explanatory keyword phrases you locate when utilizing the keyword research techniques discussed in Chapter 14. For example, as you can observe in the screenshot below, if you were creating a Manual (PPC) Sponsored Ad campaign for a "Yoga Mat Bag" product listing you would utilize the following list of search terms:

| # | | Phrase | Cerebro IQ Score | Search Volume | Sponsored ASINs |
|---|---|---|---|---|---|
| 1 | ✖ | yoga mat bag ☑ Amazon's Choice | 4,332 | 17,326 | 275 |
| 2 | ✖ | yoga bag ☑ Amazon's Choice | 551 | 11,028 | 251 |
| 3 | ✖ | yoga mat carrier ☑ Amazon's Choice | 4,860 | 4,860 | 274 |
| 4 | ✖ | yoga mat bags and carriers ☑ Amazon's Choice | 1,882 | 1,694 | 270 |
| 5 | ✖ | yoga bags and carriers for women ☑ Amazon's Choice | 1,701 | 1,308 | 0 |

Filtered keywords: 5

**1)** Yoga mat bag
**2)** Yoga bag
**3)** Yoga mat carrier
**4)** Yoga mat bags and carriers
**5)** Yoga bags and carriers for women

Total combined monthly search volume for these (5) keyword phrases is: (36,216), which means that if you utilize these specific keyword phrases in your Manual (PPC) Sponsored Ad Campaign you have the ability to reach an approximate audience total of (36,216) on a monthly basis. Ultimately, the (5) keyword phrases from the list above contains the primary terms that customers use when they are performing a search on Amazon for a "Yoga Mat Bag" therefore they should be utilized in your Manual (PPC) Sponsored Ad campaign:

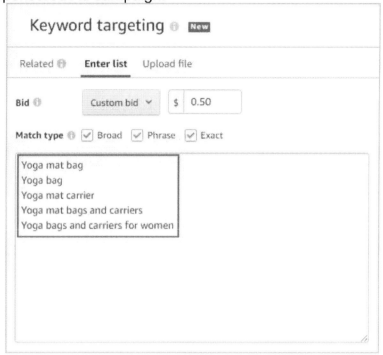

**Step #17:** Using your mouse, left-click and release on the "Add keywords" task button:

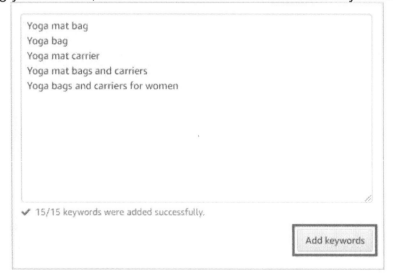

**Step #18:** Using your mouse, left-click and release on the "Launch campaign" task button to finish creating your Manual (PPC) Sponsored Ad and officially make the campaign active on Amazon:

> Launch campaign

*Note:** Please be aware, that you can opt to have your total Automatic and Manual (PPC) cost either deducted directly from your Amazon Seller Central account balance or you can pay through utilization of the designated credit card you have on file with Amazon Seller Central.

### To Designate Your Preferred Ad Cost Payment Method, follow the instructional steps included with the labeled images below:

**Step #1:** Navigate to http://sellercentral.amazon.com from within the Google Chrome Web Browser and sign into your Amazon Seller Central account.

**Step #2:** Using your mouse, without clicking, scroll over the "Settings" icon located on the top right-hand side of the Amazon Seller Central dashboard to generate a list of navigational task buttons:

> Messages | Help | Settings

**Step #3:** Using your mouse, left-click and release on the "Account Info" navigational task button located within the generated list:

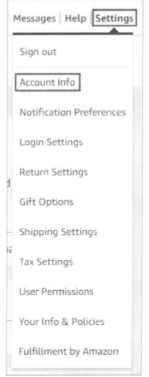

**Step #4:** Using your mouse, left-click and release on the "Charge Methods for Advertising" navigational task button:

**Step #5:** Designate which payment method you prefer to utilize for your ad cost payments:

## Running Promotional Lightning Deals & (7) Day Deals:

If your seller and product listing performance metrics are exceptional Amazon will allow you to run promotional Lightning Deals and (7) Day Deals for your product listing wherein your merchandise will be featured on Amazon's Deals page for a predetermined length of time. Utilization of this method will assist you in creating brand awareness, unloading stock, generating an influx in sales volume, and producing revenue in a brief period of time.

## Eligibility Requirements & Criteria:

- Must be a professional seller.
- Your Amazon Seller performance must have a history of receiving at least (5) Seller feedback ratings on a monthly basis.
- Your Seller Feedback rating must be at least 3.5 Stars.
- Your product listing must have a typical Product Feedback rating of at least (3) stars.
- Your product must be Prime eligible.
- Your product must be listed and sold solely in "New" condition.
- Your product must not be sold within a "Restricted" category.

## To Create & Run Promotional Lightning Deals & (7) Day Deals For Your Product Listing, follow the instructional steps included with the labeled images below:

**Step #1:** Navigate to http://sellercentral.amazon.com from within the Google Chrome Web Browser and sign into your Amazon Seller Central account.

**Step #2:** Using your mouse, without clicking, scroll over the "Advertising" icon located within the taskbar at the top of the Amazon Seller Central dashboard to generate a list of navigational task buttons:

amazon seller central    ▷    Catalog    Inventory    Pricing    Orders    Advertising    Stores    Reports    Performance    Appstore    B2B

**Step #3:** Using your mouse, left-click and release on the "Deals" navigational task button located within the generated list:

**Step #4:** Using your mouse, left-click and release on "Create a new deal" located on the right-hand side of the webpage:

**Step #5:** Choose Either The (7) day Deal Or The Lightning Deal:

## (7) Day Deal:

**Select an eligible product to run a deal on**
If you cannot find some of your products in the list below, learn how to make them eligible for deals

| | |
|---|---|
| [search box] 🔍 | Show eligible products for | Any deal type | **7-day Deals** | Lightning Deals |

## Lightning Deal:

**Select an eligible product to run a deal on**
If you cannot find some of your products in the list below, learn how to make them eligible for deals

| | |
|---|---|
| [search box] 🔍 | Show eligible products for | Any deal type | 7-day Deals | **Lightning Deals** |

**Step #6:** Schedule the deal.

**Step #7:** Configure the deal.

**Step #8:** Review & submit the deal to make it active.

## To Determine Your Total Product Listing (ACOS):

The (ACOS) can be figured by dividing the total amount you spent on advertising by the total number of units you sold. For example, if you retail a product for ($25) on Amazon and you sell a total of (1000) units then your overall revenue from those sales is ($25,000). Per say, you spent an entire grand total of ($2000) on advertising your product. You would then take ($2000/1000 Units), which equals ($2). So, your product (ACOS) is ($2) per unit.

*Understanding how to properly launch your products is another significant essential milestone to becoming and remaining a successful Amazon Seller.

# To-Do List Chapter 16:

- Generate A Coupon For Your Product Listing.
- Create & Run (1) Automatic (PPC) Sponsored Ad Campaign For Your Product Listing.
- Create & Run (1) Manual (PPC) Sponsored Ad Campaign For Your Product Listing.
- I Recommend Recording All Expenditures Associated With (ACOS): Coupons, Sponsored Ads: Automatic & Manual, (7) Day Deals, & Lightning Deals Into Your Microsoft Excel Spreadsheet Titled, "Product #1 (ACOS)," From Section 3.11.
- For Each new Product Listing You Build You Will Create A New (ACOS) Microsoft Excel Spreadsheet.

# Chapter 17:

## Amazon Brand Registry, Enhanced Brand Content, Building An Intriguing Amazon Storefront, & Brand Gating:

Brand Registry is a program that allows Amazon Sellers that are brand owners to officially register their brands specifically with Amazon. By enrolling in this exclusive program Amazon Sellers are given the ability to enhance their product listing content and the freedom to develop their brand awareness on Amazon. Furthermore, Amazon provides automatic intellectual property rights infringement protection for brands enrolled in the program as well as a set of tools that can be utilized by third-party sellers to investigate potential counterfeiters of their products.

### Benefits Of Enrolling Your Brands Into Amazon Brand Registry:

**1)** Ability to upload and add a video to your product listing. The video can be used as a means of presenting the merchandise to your customers, explaining the products usage, exhibiting the products use, and talking about the history of your brand.

**2)** Access to Amazon's A+ Content Manager which allows you to enhance your product description by giving you the ability to upload images containing your product, brand name, brand logo, as well as explanatory text highlighting positive attributes about your merchandise, brand history, and company values. Utilization of this tactic will bring an engaging professional appearance to your product detail page as well as increase your brand awareness and trust with your consumers which will lead to higher conversion rates.

**3)** Ability to design, create, and publish intriguing multi-page storefronts directly on Amazon through utilization of the Amazon Marketplace store builder. Your storefront can contain your entire product listing selection, your brand name, your brand logo, as well as explanatory text highlighting positive attributes about your merchandise, brand history, and company values. Furthermore, upon creation of your Amazon storefront you will receive your own unique www.amazon.com/yourbrandname (URL) web address which can be utilized in Amazon ads, uploaded to your company website that you created in Chapter 7, and used in social media marketing campaigns, such as Facebook ads, to guide consumers directly to your product listings.

**To Navigate To The Amazon Storefront Creator, follow the instructional steps included with the labeled images below:**

**Step #1:** Navigate to http://sellercentral.amazon.com from within the Google Chrome Web Browser and sign into your Amazon Seller Central account.

**Step #2:** Using your mouse, without clicking, scroll over the "Stores" icon located within the taskbar at the top of the Amazon Seller Central dashboard to generate a list containing a navigational task button:

| amazon seller central | ▷ | Catalog | Inventory | Pricing | Orders | Advertising | Stores | Reports | Performance | Appstore | B2B |

**Step #3:** Using your mouse, left-click and release on the "Manage Stores" navigational task button located within the generated list:

**Step #4:** Using your mouse, left-click and release on the "Create Store" navigational task button:

Create Store  >

**4)** Ability to create and run specialized sponsored brand focused headline ads related to a customer's particular keyword search. These type of headline ads can contain your brand logo, brand name, and up to (3) product listings. The ad is typically located at the top of the 1st page of keyword related searches. When a customer clicks on your brand logo they are directed to your associated Amazon storefront. When a customer clicks on one of your (3) product listings from within the headline ad they are directed to your product detail page for the specific merchandise they chose to view.

**To Navigate To The Sponsored Brand Ad Campaign Creator, follow the instructional steps included with the labeled images below:**

**Step #1:** Navigate to http://sellercentral.amazon.com from within the Google Chrome Web Browser and sign into your Amazon Seller Central account.

**Step #2:** Using your mouse, without clicking, scroll over the "Advertising" icon located within the taskbar at the top of the Amazon Seller Central dashboard to generate a list of navigational task buttons:

**Step #3:** Using your mouse, left-click and release on the "Campaign Manager" navigational task button located within the generated list:

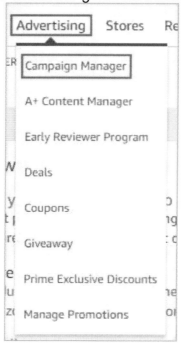

**Step #4:** Using your mouse, left-click and release on the "Continue" navigational task button:

**5)** Ability to create and run specialized sponsored brand focused display ads for your merchandise outside of the Amazon platform to drive external traffic to your Amazon product listing detail pages.

**To Navigate To The Sponsored Display Ad Campaign Creator, follow the instructional steps included with the labeled images below:**

**Step #1:** Navigate to http://sellercentral.amazon.com from within the Google Chrome Web Browser and sign into your Amazon Seller Central account.

**Step #2:** Using your mouse, without clicking, scroll over the "Advertising" icon located within the taskbar at the top of the Amazon Seller Central dashboard to generate a list of navigational task buttons:

**Step #3:** Using your mouse, left-click and release on the "Campaign Manager" navigational task button located within the generated list:

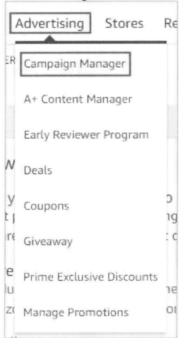

**Step #4:** Using your mouse, left-click and release on the "Continue" navigational task button:

**6)** Ability to apply directly with Amazon Seller Support to get your enrolled brand's (ASINs) gated. If Amazon approves your request then no other unauthorized third-party sellers can retail your particular branded products on your product listings without your prior consent ultimately preventing hijackers and snipers.

**7)** Access to the Brand Dashboard within your Amazon Seller Central account which is a tool that allows you to track your specific brands consumer traffic and conversion progress. When issues arise, the tool will then help you to recognize opportunities to optimize the customer experience with your brand in an attempt to increase sales volume.

**8)** Access to the Amazon Brand Registry Support team which you can contact for assistance related to intellectual property rights infringement and brand protection issues.

**9)** Access to the set of (3) search and report tools to investigate and identify potential threats to your brand and counterfeiters of your products:

- Global Search
- Image Search
- Bulk (ASIN) Search

**10)** Access to automatic intellectual property rights infringement protection from Amazon for your enrolled brands.

Amazon works to identify and prevent third-party sellers from utilizing your enrolled brands:

- Trademarked brand name in their product listing titles.
- Product listing images containing your brand name and brand logo.
- Product listings being created with your brand name.

## The Current Countries In Which Amazon Brand Registry Is Available For Third-Party Sellers Are:

### North America:

- United States: www.amazon.com
- Mexico: www.amazon.com.mx
- Canada: www.amazon.ca

### Oceania:

- Australia: www.amazon.com.au

### South America:

- Brazil: www.amazon.com.br

### Europe:

- United Kingdom: www.amazon.co.uk
- Spain: www.amazon.es
- Italy: www.amazon.it
- Germany: www.amazon.de
- France: www.amazon.fr

### Asia:

- United Arab Emirates: www.amazon.ae
- Turkey: www.amazon.com.tr
- Japan: www.amazon.co.jp
- India: www.amazon.in

## Eligibility Requirements For Brand Enrollment Into Amazon Brand Registry:

**1)** You must have a federally registered trademark for your brand name officially obtained from the country in which you retail your merchandise on the Amazon Marketplace as was discussed in Chapter 9, Section 9.6. For example, if you sell on www.amazon.com and you intend on enrolling your brand into the registry program for this specific Amazon Marketplace then you will require an active federally registered trademark for your brand name obtained from the (USPTO) in the United States.

**2)** Your brand name must be visibly printed on your individual product packaging as was discussed in Chapter 9, Section 9.7.

**3)** Your brand name must be visibly printed directly on your product as was discussed in Chapter 9, Section 9.7.

### To Enroll A Brand Into The Amazon Brand Registry Program, follow the instructional steps included with the labeled images below:

**Step #1:**

#### Make Sure You Have The Following List Of Items Readily Available:

- Your Brand Name.
- Your Associated Brand Name Government-Registered Trademark Number.
- One Image Of Your Individual Product Packaging Containing Your Trademarked Brand Name.
- One Image Of Your Product Containing Your Trademarked Brand Name.

**Step #2:** Navigate to http://sellercentral.amazon.com from within the Google Chrome Web Browser and sign into your Amazon Seller Central account.

**Step #3:** Using your mouse, without clicking, scroll over the "Advertising" icon located within the taskbar at the top of the Amazon Seller Central dashboard to generate a list of navigational task buttons:

**Step #4:** Using your mouse, left-click and release on the "A+ Content Manager" navigational task button located within the generated list:

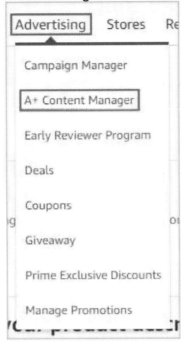

**Step #5:** Using your mouse, left-click and release on the "Get Started Registering Your Brand" navigational task button:

Get Started Registering Your Brand

**Step #6:** Using your mouse, left-click and release on the "Get Started" navigational task button:

Get started >

**Step #7:** Using your mouse, left-click and release on the "Enroll now" navigational task button:

Enroll now >

**Step #8:** Select the country-specific marketplace that you have an active registered trademark and want to enroll your brands. For example, if you have an active registered trademark in the United States and you sell on the www.amazon.com marketplace you would select the United States icon.

**Step #9:** Sign into Amazon Brand Registry utilizing the same credentials you used to create your Amazon Seller Central account within Chapter 11.

**Step #10:** Using your mouse, left-click and release on the "Enroll a new brand" navigational task button:

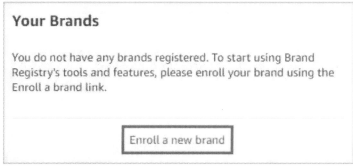

**Step #11:** Fill out the Amazon Brand Registry application specific to the brand you are enrolling into the program.

*Note: Please be aware that Brand Registry approval is not instantaneous. Once you finish the application process be prepared to wait approximately (24-48) hours to for Amazon to review your application and approve your enrolled brands.

*Understanding the importance of enrolling your brands into Amazon's Brand Registry program is another significant essential milestone to becoming and remaining a successful Amazon Seller.

## To-Do List Chapter 17:

- o I Recommend Enrolling All Brands You Design & Trademark Into The Amazon Brand Registry Program.

# Chapter 18:

## Product Reviews, Star Ratings, Third-Party Seller Feedback, & Customer Service Practices:

I will reiterate the review ideology that was discussed in Chapter 8, which is the fact that customers buying products on Amazon typically tend to rely heavily on reading previous customer's product reviews to help guide them in their purchasing decision. This means that when a consumer is searching for a specific product to purchase they are much more inclined to buy their merchandise from a seller's listing that has a high-review count in contrast to procuring their goods from a seller with a low-review count. Furthermore, customers buying products on Amazon also tend to rely on previous customers star rating values to help guide them in their purchasing decision. Ultimately, a products star rating value acts either as a persuasive hook that draws a customer into viewing your Amazon listing or as a dissuasive deterrent that will discourage them from viewing your Amazon listing. A high (4-5) star rating value will act as a persuasive hook that draws customers into viewing your product listing. On the contrary, a low (1-2) star rating value will act as a dissuasive deterrent that will discourage customers from viewing your product listing. Try to perceive customer star rating values from a consumer's perspective. Would you choose to view and purchase a product from an Amazon Seller who has a low negative (1-2) star rating value for their product listing or would you opt to view and purchase a similar product from an Amazon seller who has a high positive (4-5) star rating value for their product listing? Additionally, Amazon consumers can opt to leave feedback directly on your product listing in regard to your customer service practices as a third-party Amazon Seller. What this means to you as an Amazon Seller is that to procure sales, rank to the top of page one, and dominate the category you are retailing within you must attempt to receive positive reviews, high-star rating values, as well as optimistic third-party seller feedback from your customers for your product listings. This subject can be confusing, daunting, and challenging for some Amazon Sellers new to this process. Therefore, to alleviate the stressfulness often associated with the mechanics involved with this topic I have broken this chapter down into **(6)** methods that you can utilize to procure positive authentic product listing reviews, high-star rating values, and optimistic third-party seller feedback from your Amazon customers.

Before we delve into the following **(6)** review method tutorials you must first understand Amazon's (TOS) policies in regard to what are acceptable and unacceptable practices and methods of acquiring reviews.

## Acceptable Authentic Review Practices & Methods:

- Partaking in Amazon's (ERP) Early Reviewer Program.
- Placing a promotional business card product insert into your individual product packaging that kindly asks the customer to write an honest product review and rate their experience for their purchase from your company directly on your Amazon product listing.
- Sending one post purchase follow-up email through your Amazon Seller Central account to your customer that kindly asks them to write an honest product review and rate their experience for their purchase from your company directly on your Amazon product listing.

## Unacceptable Unauthentic Review Manipulation Practices & Methods:

- Offering an incentive to your customers, such as money, your product for free, a discount, a coupon, a gift, or free merchandise prior or post purchase in exchange for a written review and star rating for your product listing.
- Making review suggestions, such as asking for a positive review and high-star rating from your customers on your promotional business card product insert or within your post purchase follow-up email. When utilizing these (2) methods I would instead recommend utilizing the word honest in place of the word positive.
- Harassing your customers by continually sending more than one post purchase email requesting them to write a review and rate your product listing ultimately spamming them.
- Paying product reviewers and marketing influencers to purchase your product in order to write reviews and leave star ratings for your product listings.
- Having individuals, such as family, friends, co-workers, and employees write a review and leave a star rating for your product listing.
- Asking a customer to remove or alter a negative review and low-star rating into a positive review and high-star rating.
- Creating an Amazon buyer account, purchasing your own merchandise, and writing reviews for your product listings.
- Creating an Amazon buyer account, purchasing your competitor's merchandise, and writing negative reviews for their product listings in attempt to tarnish their reputation.

*Cautionary Note: If you do utilize the unacceptable review manipulation practices and methods stated above you run the risk of having your product listing reviews and star ratings deleted, your product listings suspended, or your Amazon Seller Central account adjourned until the issues have been addressed through communication with Amazon. Furthermore, if you then continue to disobey Amazon's (TOS) regarding their review manipulation policies they will close your Amazon Seller Central account and indefinitely ban you from retailing your products on the Amazon Marketplace.

**I Recommend Concurrently Utilizing The Following (5) Methods To Acquire Positive Authentic Product Listing Reviews, High-Star Rating Values, & Optimistic Third-Party Seller Feedback From Your Amazon Customers:**

**Method #1:** Retailing High-Quality Merchandise At A Reasonable Product Price Point:

The primary key component in procuring positive authentic product listing reviews and high-star rating values from your Amazon customers relies heavily on the quality of your merchandise and your product price points. If you retail a well-manufactured product constructed with durable high-quality materials at a reasonable price point then customers will be much more apt to log into their Amazon account to write a positive review and leave a high (4-5) star rating on your product listing. On the contrary, if you sell sub-standard poorly manufactured products constructed with easily breakable low-quality materials then you can expect customers to write negative reviews and leave low (1-2) star ratings on your product listing. Therefore, to receive excellent reviews and a high-star ratings for your product listings I recommend solely selling sturdy well-constructed merchandise at a sensible price that is both fair for you and for your customers.

**Method #2:** Enrolling Your (SKUs) In Amazon's Early Reviewer Program:

For a fee of ($60) per, you can opt to enroll your (SKUs) into the Early Reviewer Program which is an incentivized review service designed and offered by Amazon that will assist you in acquiring up to (5) authentic customer reviews and star ratings for your product listings. Once you have enrolled a (SKU) in the program then Amazon will choose, at random, up to (5) customers who have purchased your merchandise to write an honest authentic review and leave a star rating directly on your product listing in exchange for a ($3) Amazon gift card.

**Important Information Regarding Amazon's Early Reviewer Program:**

- The program is currently only offered for Amazon Sellers who are retailing their products on the (USA) Amazon Marketplace via www.amazon.com.
- The program will continue to petition reviews from customers who have purchased your product until you acquire a total of (5) incentivized reviews for your product listing or for a period of (1) year, whichever comes first.
- You are not charged the ($60) per (SKU) enrollment fee until you receive your first incentivized customer review from the program. If you receive no incentivized customer reviews for a period of one year then you will not be charged for the program and will be automatically unenrolled.
- Organically obtained customer reviews do not count towards your (5) incentivized customer reviews while your (SKU) is enrolled in the program, which means that if you enroll your (SKU) into the program and begin receiving organic customer reviews that total more than (5) Amazon will still continue to request up to (5) incentivized reviews from customers who have purchased your product.

- Solely Stand-Alone SKUs and Parent SKUs are eligible for enrollment into the program. If you have a Parent (SKU) then the Children (SKUs) will automatically be enrolled with the Parent (SKU) and the (5) incentivized customer reviews will be shared between them.
- You and your product listing customers will be able to identify that a review has been incentivized by Amazon due to the review containing an orange badge that reads "Early Reviewer Rewards."
- Amazon Sellers are not allowed to modify incentivized reviews by communicating with customers about the reviews written and retrieved through the use of the Early Reviewer Program.

## Requirements:

- You must have your Brand Registered with Amazon (Chapter 17).
- You must have trademark ownership of the brand name that is printed on your product and its product packaging in relation to the (SKU) you are enrolling into the Early Reviewer Program.
- In order for your (SKU) to be eligible for enrollment into the program you must currently have less than (5) customer reviews for the specific product listing.
- To be eligible for enrollment in the program your retail product listing price point must be above ($9).

**To Enroll Your (SKUs) Into Amazon's Early Reviewer Program, follow the instructional steps included with the labeled images below:**

**Step #1:** Navigate to http://sellercentral.amazon.com from within the Google Chrome Web Browser and log into your Amazon Seller Central account.

**Step #2:** Using your mouse, scroll without clicking over the Advertising tab located at the top of the Amazon Seller Central dashboard to generate a list of navigational task buttons:

| amazon seller central | ▷ | Catalog | Inventory | Pricing | Orders | Advertising | Stores | Reports | Performance | Appstore | B2B |

**Step #3:** Using your mouse, left-click and release on the "Early Reviewer Program" navigational task button:

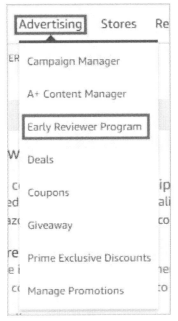

**Step #4:** Using your mouse, left-click and release on the "Enroll in Program" navigational task button located at the top left-hand side of the screen within the Early Reviewer Program's taskbar:

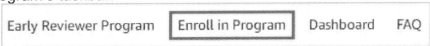

**Step #5:** As you can observe in the screenshot below, in the center of the screen is a section that allows you to individually enter the (SKUs) you wish to enroll in the program. After you have entered your desired (SKU) you will use your mouse to left-click and release on the "Check Availability" navigational task button:

## OR:

       *If you have numerous (SKUs) to enroll you can opt to create a (CSV) template spreadsheet utilizing Microsoft Excel that contains a list of all the (SKUs) you wish to enroll in the Early Reviewer Program. As you can observe in the screenshot below, you will utilize the "Bulk Upload Enrollment" navigational button located within the "Enroll in Program" section form the previous Step #4:

## To Navigate To The Enrollment Dashboard, follow the instructional steps included with the labeled images below:

       Once your (SKUs) have been accepted to the Early Reviewer Program you can easily track each (SKUs) incentivized review progress from your Amazon Seller Central account within the Enrollment Dashboard.

**Step #1:** Navigate to http://sellercentral.amazon.com from within the Google Chrome Web Browser and log into your Amazon Seller Central account.

**Step #2:** Using your mouse, scroll without clicking over the Advertising tab located at the top of the Amazon Seller Central dashboard to generate a list of navigational task buttons:

**amazon** seller central    ▷    Catalog    Inventory    Pricing    Orders    Advertising    Stores    Reports    Performance    Appstore    B2B

**Step #3:** Using your mouse, left-click and release on the "Early Reviewer Program" navigational task button:

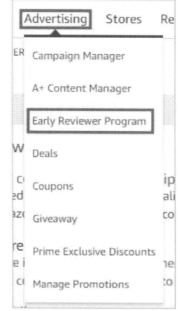

**Step #4:** Using your mouse, left-click and release on the "Dashboard" navigational task button located at the top left-hand side of the screen within the Early Reviewer Program's taskbar:

| Early Reviewer Program | Enroll in Program | Dashboard | FAQ |

**Method #3:** Promotional Business Card Product Insert:

As you can observe in the following (2) example images below, you can opt to utilize Adobe Illustrator, (Chapter 9, Section 9.6), to design a business card that can be inserted into your individual product packaging that promotes your company as well as thanks the customer for their purchase while simultaneously asking them to write an honest review and leave a star rating for your product listing on Amazon.

**Image #1:** As you can observe in the image below, to promote your company and brand I recommend printing your primary company name and brand logo on the frontside of the business card:

**Image #2:** As you can observe in the image below, on the backside of the business card I recommend first showing your appreciation to the customer while simultaneously promoting your primary company name. I then suggest kindly asking satisfied customers to support your company and share their experience with other customers by writing an honest review on Amazon for their specific purchase from your company. You can then opt to write a brief paragraph outlining the fact that if the customer has a problem with their order they can contact your company to address the issue which will hopefully dissuade them from instantly writing a negative review before first communicating with you to fix the error. At the very bottom of the business card product insert I have printed (5) stars which is a symbolic manner of asking the customer on a subconscious level for a (5) star rating without actually writing the words due to the latter being suggestively unacceptable by Amazon's (TOS).

## (4) Cost-Effective Methods For Printing Your Business Card Product Inserts:

Once you finish designing your business card product insert (AF) Art File you will need to locate a company that can perform the printing service for you.

**1)** Some manufacturers have the capabilities required to print business cards at a low per unit cost. Therefore, I recommend initially asking your primary product or individual product packaging supplier if they can print your business cards for you. If they can perform the service, you will first discuss and negotiate the price of a mass order. Once you come to an agreement on the cost you will then provide them with your business card (AF) Art File so that they can print your exact design specifications.

**2)** If your supplier does not have the capabilities required to print the business cards you can opt to ask them to refer you to a reputable low-cost high-quality printing company that can perform the service for you.

**3)** You can locate various printing companies on the Alibaba Marketplace platform via www.alibaba.com utilizing the supplier research, communication, and negotiation techniques discussed in Chapter 9.

**4)** You can provide your business card (AF) Art File to a printing company, such as, Vistaprint via www.vistaprint.com and they can perform the service for you.

*****Note:** If you feel that learning Adobe Illustrator and creating the graphics for your business card product insert is unfeasible or simply not appealing to you, you can choose to outsource your design work by hiring a professional graphic designer online.

**To Outsource & Hire A Professional Photo Editor Refer To Any Of The Websites Below From Within The Google Chrome Web Browser:**

- Bookmark #17: www.peopleperhour.com
- Bookmark #18: www.upwork.com
- Bookmark #19: www.fiverr.com
- Bookmark #20: www.freelancer.com
- Bookmark #21: www.99designs.com

**Method #4:** Sending A Post Purchase Follow-Up Email To The Customer:

After your Amazon customers have received their merchandise I recommend sending one follow-up email thanking them for their purchase and kindly asking them write a review and rate their experience directly on your product listing. For your post purchase follow-up email, I recommend using similar wording as the business card product insert example from the previous Method #3. A time effective and efficient way to perform this task is through utilization of an automated email service, such as Follow-Up offered by Helium 10.

*****Note:** Amazon automatically notifies each consumer when their order has been shipped and delivered therefore it is unnecessary for you to follow-up through email post purchase with your customers in regard to either of these topics.

**<u>To Navigate To Helium 10's Follow-Up Tool & Learn How To Effectively Utilize The Software, follow the instructional steps included with the labeled images below:</u>**

**<u>Step #1:</u>** Navigate to <u>www.helium10.com</u> from within the Google Chrome Web Browser, sign into your account, and be sure that you have granted Helium 10 (MWS) access to your Amazon Seller Central account as was discussed in Chapter 12.

**<u>Step #2:</u>** Using your mouse, left-click and release on the tool's icon located on the top right-hand side of the Helium 10 dashboard to generate a list of navigational task buttons:

**<u>Step #3:</u>** Using your mouse, left-click and release on the Helium 10 Follow-Up tool located within the generated list of navigational task buttons to navigate to the Follow-Up dashboard:

*You have now been navigated to the Helium 10 Follow-Up Dashboard which you will utilize to track your overall merchant to buyer contact history. Furthermore, on the left-hand side of the screen you can locate the navigational taskbar containing the tools you will utilize for all of your post purchase customer follow-up necessities including viewing your product listing orders, setting up automated email sequences, creating email templates, blacklisting customers you no longer wish to contact via email, and altering your settings.

**Image:** Follow-Up Task Bar:

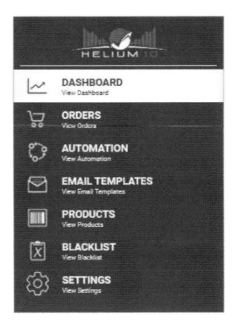

❖ I highly recommend completing the following Step #4 which entails watching the provided tutorials on how to effectively utilize Helium 10's customer Follow-Up tool.

**Step #4:** Using your mouse, left-click and release on the white "Learn" icon located on the top left-hand side of the screen to navigate to the Follow-Up tutorials:

**Method #5:** Running Special Deals & Creating Promotions:

You can opt to run special deals, generate coupons, partake in Amazon's giveaway program, and create promotions for your product listings through your Amazon Seller Central account as was discussed in Chapter 16. By utilizing this method, you will potentially hook a larger number of customers than usual and observe an influx in sales volume which will increase the likelihood of receiving customer reviews as well as star ratings for your product listing.

**Method #6:** Lowering Your Product Price Point:

If the (5) methods discussed above do not produce the desired results, you can opt to competitively decrease your overall product listing price point from its typical retail amount for a short period of time. By reducing the price of your merchandise, you will potentially hook a larger number of customers than usual and observe an influx in sales volume which will increase the likelihood of receiving customer reviews as well as star ratings for your product listing.

## Professionally Dealing With Negative Product Listing Reviews & Low-Star Ratings:

Although you may retail well-manufactured merchandise constructed with durable high-quality materials at a reasonable price point you will typically still encounter scenarios where you have dissatisfied customers who will write negative reviews and leave low-star ratings on your product listings. Having a few customers who disapprove of your product is inevitably common and just part of being in business as an Amazon Seller. No matter what you do to fix an issue with particular customers they will remain impossible to please. On the contrary, depending on the severity of the customer's complaint, through performing a specific review related customer service practice you can change some upsets customers into satisfied ones. Amazon's (TOS) forbids you from asking a customer to remove or alter a negative review into a positive review but they do allow you to contact the buyer who wrote the negative review through your Seller Central account to correct the problem the consumer is experiencing with your product. Although you cannot directly ask a buyer to change a review, if you reach out to them to address an issue and fix a problem, the customer will typically remove their negative review entirely or at the very least change their damaging review into a more optimistic one on their own behalf. When you do contact a buyer in association with a negative review be sure to do so in a timely, respectful, and professional manner that thoroughly addresses the customer's complaints in direct correlation to their written review.

## To Contact A Buyer Through Your Amazon Seller Central Account, follow the instructional steps included with the labeled images below:

**Step #1:** Navigate to http://sellercentral.amazon.com from within the Google Chrome Web Browser and sign into your Amazon Seller Central account.

**Step #2:** Using your mouse, without clicking, scroll over the "Orders" icon located within the taskbar at the top of the Amazon Seller Central dashboard to generate a list of navigational task buttons:

**Step #3:** Using your mouse, left-click and release on the "Manage Orders" navigational task button located within the generated list:

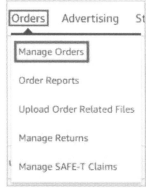

**Step #4:** From within your list of orders locate the buyer you wish to contact in association with the negative review on your product listing.

**Step #5:** Using your mouse, left-click and release on the name of the buyer located within the "Order Details" column to navigate to the "Contact Buyer" page.

**Step #6:** From the "Contact Buyer" page select the reason for contacting the customer.

**Step #7:** Write your message in the provided area.

**Step #8:** Using your mouse, left-click and release on the "Send" button.

## How To Utilize Negative Reviews To Your Advantage:

In some cases, negative reviews can be a helpful tool that you can utilize to gain insight into what you are doing wrong and what could be changed to make your product better, optimize your product listing to be more informative, or make the buying experience more pleasant for your customers. For example, if numerous customers are complaining within their product reviews that their order did not come with directions on how to use or care for the merchandise you could opt to create, print, and add an insertable instructional booklet to place inside your individual packaging.

## (2) Recommended Solutions To Utilize If Your Negative Reviews Far Outweigh Your Positive Reviews Thus, Resulting In No Sales:

If you encounter this unfortunate scenario there (2) recommended solutions you can utilize to resolve the issue:

## Solution #1:

You can attempt to quickly sell your entire problematic stock by drastically lowering your product listing price point down to your initial product investment and production cost. Once you sell your remaining units and regain your initial investment cost you will then permanently delete the product listing. You will then address the negative reviews, fix the issues with the product, and have an improved version of your initial product manufactured. You will then build a new product listing for the merchandise and relist the improved version under a new (ASIN), ultimately starting afresh. Another option would be to accept this unfortunate scenario as a learning experience, move on from the problematic product listing, and alternatively spend your time researching an entirely different type of merchandise to sell on Amazon.

## Solution #2:

If utilization of Method #1 is not resolving the issue I recommend having your entire stock of problematic merchandise shipped back to you from the Amazon Product Fulfillment Center (FBA Only), permanently deleting the product listing, attempting to regain your initial investment by retailing your remaining stock singly or wholesale on another online marketplace platform, such as eBay or AliExpress, and discovering a different type of merchandise to sell on Amazon, ultimately starting afresh.

## Professionally Dealing With Negative Third-Party Seller Customer Feedback:

Although you may have exceptional customer service practices, the condition of the product was excellent when sent out to the consumer, the packaging was undamaged, and your product listing description is accurate you will typically still encounter scenarios where you have dissatisfied customers who will write negative seller feedback on your product listings. Having a few customers who disapprove of your post purchase customer service practices and the condition of their order is inevitably common and just part of being in business as an Amazon Seller. Seller feedback is similar to product reviews in the sense that no matter what you do to fix an issue with particular customers they will remain impossible to please. On the contrary, depending on the severity of the customer's complaint, through performing a specific seller feedback customer service practice you can change some upsets customers into satisfied ones. Amazon's (TOS) forbids you from asking a customer to remove or alter negative seller feedback into positive seller feedback but they do allow you to contact the buyer who wrote the negative seller feedback through your Seller Central account to correct the problem the consumer is experiencing. Although you cannot directly ask a buyer to change seller feedback, if you reach out to them to address an issue and fix a problem, the customer will typically remove their negative seller feedback entirely or at the very least change their damaging feedback into optimistic feedback on their own behalf. When you do contact a buyer in association with negative seller feedback be sure to do so in a timely, respectful, and professional manner that thoroughly addresses the customer's complaints in direct correlation to their seller feedback.

Furthermore, you can opt to publicly reply to the negative seller feedback in direct correlation with the specific feedback posting. This means that customers that view your Amazon Seller Profile Page will be able to observe your response to the negative feedback. Ultimately, your exceptional customer service performance will show the current consumer who wrote the negative feedback as well as future buyers that you are readily available and that your company cares about their seller feedback. When you do post a public response be sure to do so in a timely, respectful, and professional manner that thoroughly addresses the customer's complaints in direct correlation to their seller feedback. Please be aware that customers cannot reply to your public response to seller feedback therefore if you wish to exchange messages with a consumer about negative seller feedback you will need to individually contact the buyer as discussed in the previous paragraph.

**To Track Performance, Manage, & Respond To Your Third-Party Customer Seller Feedback, follow the instructional steps included with the labeled images below:**

**Step #1:** Navigate to http://sellercentral.amazon.com from within the Google Chrome Web Browser and sign into your Amazon Seller Central account.

**Step #2:** Using your mouse, without clicking, scroll over the "Performance" icon located within the taskbar at the top of the Amazon Seller Central dashboard to generate a list of navigational task buttons:

**Step #3:** Using your mouse, left-click and release on the "Feedback" navigational task button located within the generated list:

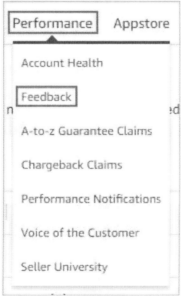

❖ You have now been navigated to the "Feedback Manager" within Amazon Seller Central where you can manage, track performance, and respond to feedback.

**How To Utilize Negative Third-Party Customer Seller Feedback To Your Advantage:**

In some cases, negative customer seller feedback can be a helpful tool that you can utilize to gain insight into what you are doing wrong and what could be changed to better your customer service practices, alter your product packaging to be more durable, or optimize the accuracy of your product listing description to make the buying experience more pleasant for your customers. For example, if numerous customers are complaining within their seller feedback that your product description is mistakenly mis-representing your merchandise you can easily alter your product listing within your Amazon Seller Central account to make it more detailed, informative, and accurate.

## Performing Customer Service Tasks As An Amazon Seller:

      Amazon's (TOS) requires you to respond to all customer emails received through your Amazon Seller Central account within (24) hours therefore I recommend navigating to the message center at least once a day, diligently reading through your customer to buyer emails, and replying to any customer notifications that require a response. When you do respond be sure to do so in a timely, respectful, and professional manner that thoroughly answers or addresses the customers questions or concerns. By replying to your customer's messages in this fashion you have the potential to help your company avoid receival of unnecessary product returns, negative product listing reviews, low-star ratings, and damaging seller feedback. Furthermore, satisfied customers who receive exceptional customer service when they have a question or concern are much more apt to write a positive product listing review, rate their experience with a high-star, and leave optimistic seller feedback thus resulting in exponential growth in your sales volume by drawing new consumers into your product listing.

## To Check Your Messages & Respond To Customers Within Amazon Seller Central, follow the instructional steps included with the labeled images below:

**Step #1:** Navigate to http://sellercentral.amazon.com from within the Google Chrome Web Browser and sign into your Amazon Seller Central account.

**Step #2:** Using your mouse, left-click and release on the "Messages" task button located on the top right-hand side of the Amazon Seller Central dashboard to navigate to the message center:

❖ You have now been navigated to the message center within Amazon Seller Central. If a response to a customer email is required you will be automatically notified upon arrival to the message center and you can easily reply to the buyer directly from this section of your Amazon Seller Central account.

**\*Note:** If you begin to receive the same question from several buyers in relation to a particular product listing or your customer service practices, and the inquiry requires the same repeated response to each customer I recommend utilizing the email template tool located within your Amazon Seller Central message center. This time saving tool allows you to build an email template that can be utilized as a quick response to frequently asked questions in contrast to you having to repeatedly type the same reply to numerous customers.

**To Locate & Utilize The Email Template Tool, follow the instructional steps included with the labeled images below:**

**Step #1:** Navigate to http://sellercentral.amazon.com from within the Google Chrome Web Browser and sign into your Amazon Seller Central account.

**Step #2:** Using your mouse, left-click and release on the "Messages" task button located on the top right-hand side of the Amazon Seller Central dashboard to navigate to the message center:

**Step #3:** Using your mouse, left-click and release on the "Manage E-mail Templates" navigational task button located on the top right-hand side of the message center:

Links ▼

Messaging Permissions
Manage E-mail Templates

**Step #4:** Using your mouse, left-click and release on the "Create Template" navigational task button:

**Step #5:** Name your email template, insert a placeholder, and write the frequently required response. Then using your mouse, left-click and release on the "Save" button to finish creating your email template:

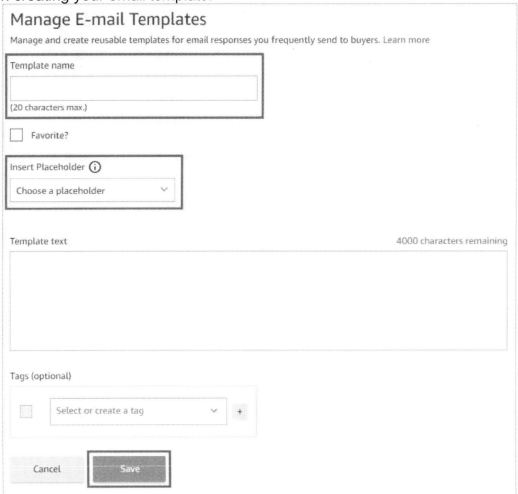

**To Utilize Your Email Template, follow the instructional steps included with the labeled images below:**

**Step #1:** Navigate to http://sellercentral.amazon.com from within the Google Chrome Web Browser and sign into your Amazon Seller Central account.

**Step #2:** Using your mouse, left-click and release on the "Messages" task button located on the top right-hand side of the Amazon Seller Central dashboard to navigate to the message center:

**Step #3:** Locate the customer message that requires your created email template response.

**Step #4:** Using your mouse, left-click and release on the "Select Template" button located above the "Reply" box to generate a list of the email templates you have created.

**Step #5:** Choose the email template you wish to utilize for your response, and you will now observe that the email template text appears in the "Reply" box.

**Step #6:** Using your mouse, left-click and release on the "Reply" button to send the response to the customer.

**To Edit Or Delete An Email Template You Created, follow the instructional steps included with the labeled images below:**

**Step #1:** Navigate to http://sellercentral.amazon.com from within the Google Chrome Web Browser and sign into your Amazon Seller Central account.

**Step #2:** Using your mouse, left-click and release on the "Messages" task button located on the top right-hand side of the Amazon Seller Central dashboard to navigate to the message center:

**Step #3:** Using your mouse, left-click and release on the "Manage E-mail Templates" navigational task button located on the top right-hand side of the message center:

**Step #4:** Using your mouse, left-click and release on either the "Edit" or "Delete" navigational task buttons located within the "Actions" list to alter or permanently remove the email template:

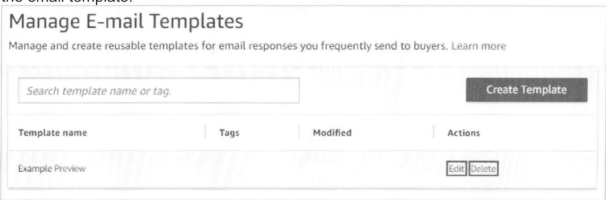

## Utilizing The (Q&A) Section Of Your Product Listing:

      Another method of performing customer service is through utilization of the (Q&A) section of your product listings. The (Q&A) section is automatically set up for each product listing you create, and it is there for customers to use when they have a question regarding your specific product. When you receive a question in this section of your product listings you will instantaneously be notified through the message center of your Amazon Seller Central account. I recommend routinely checking the message center for these types of notifications and when you do receive a question on your product listing answer it in a timely, respectful, professional and thorough manner. Your exceptional customer service performance will show the current consumer as well as future buyers that you are readily available and that your company cares about their questions. Furthermore, if this is a buyer who has not yet purchased your product then your quick detailed response to their question may result in a new sale. On the contrary, if this is a current customer your timely comprehensive response to their question could result in them writing a positive product listing review, rating their experience with a high-star, and leaving optimistic seller feedback thus resulting in exponential growth in your sales volume by drawing new consumers into your product listing.

**Image:** (Q&A) Section Of A Product Listing Observed From A Customer's Perspective:

      *Understanding the importance of customer feedback is another significant essential milestone to becoming and remaining a successful Amazon Seller.

# Chapter 19:

## Product Returns & Replacement Orders:

If you retail well-manufactured merchandise constructed with durable high-quality materials at a reasonable price point then customers will be much less apt to return their products. On the contrary, if you sell sub-standard poorly manufactured products constructed with easily breakable low-quality materials then you can expect a high-return rate. Having a high-return rate can negatively affect your product listing rank position and at the very worst your overall reputation with Amazon which could lead to Seller Central account suspension. Therefore, to avoid a high-return rate I recommend solely retailing sturdy well-constructed merchandise at a sensible price that is both fair for you and for your customers.

Although you may retail well-manufactured merchandise constructed with durable high-quality materials at a reasonable price point you will typically still have some customers opt to return your product for one reason or another. Do not be disheartened by a few product returns due to the fact that it is inevitably common and merely part of being in business as an Amazon Seller. Since you will most likely be encountering product returns you must learn how to properly set-up, edit your preferences, process, and manage them as a third-party seller which relies heavily on first understanding Amazon's customer return policies.

### Amazon's Customer Return Policies:

### (FBA)

When a customer orders a product from a third-party seller via (FBA) the consumer is automatically given a (30) day grace period in which they can opt to return the merchandise in exchange for a full refund with exception to non-returnable items, such as fresh flowers, live indoor plants, and edibles. When a customer chooses to return an item, they are first reimbursed for their purchase, and they are then given a timeline of (45) days to ship the product back to the Amazon Fulfilment Center. If they fail to return the merchandise within the allotted time they will be recharged the initial price they paid for their order.

*Note: Please be aware, that the return grace period for customers who purchase their products via (FBA) during the holiday shopping season is extended. This means that customers who purchase your products via (FBA) between the dates of November 1st and December 31st are allowed to return the merchandise until January 31st.

## (FBM)

When a customer orders a product via (FBM) due to Amazon's (TOS) the third-party seller is obligated to offer the consumer the favorable (30) day grace period in which they can opt to return the merchandise in exchange for a full refund. When a buyer opts to return merchandise in exchange for a refund, unless otherwise stated, they are required to first ship the product back to the third-party seller's provided return address prior to receival of their monetary reimbursement. If the customer fails to return the merchandise the third-party seller is not obligated to reimburse the buyer for their purchase.

## (FBA) Product Return Policies & Management For Amazon Sellers:

When utilizing (FBA) as your product fulfilment method Amazon will automatically take care of each aspect of the customer return process for you including reimbursing the customer's funds, offering them a shipping label via their buyer account to ship the merchandise back to the Amazon Fulfilment Center it originated from, and arranging shipment of the product via courier from the consumer's address. When your returned merchandise arrives back to the Amazon Product Fulfilment Center the (FBA) warehouse staff will determine the condition of the product. If Amazon deems the product as being in sellable condition the merchandise will be returned to your active purchasable inventory. If the product is deemed as unsellable the merchandise will not be returned to your purchasable inventory and will appear as unfulfillable within your Amazon Seller Central account. Please note that you are still being charged typical monthly storage rates for returned unfulfillable merchandise and it is your responsibility to manage this type of inventory through utilization of your Amazon Seller Central account. There are (2) circumstantial options for handling unfulfillable merchandise that rely on who is considered to be at fault when the product is deemed unsellable.

If the reason the merchandise is deemed unfulfillable by Amazon's (FBA) warehouse staff is due to a product or its individual product packaging being "Defective" or incurring "Customer Damage" this means that either you or your customer is at fault. In either of these scenarios you will be required to request the removal of the unfulfillable merchandise. There are two options for removing your unfulfillable inventory. You can either request Amazon to dispose of it for you or you can opt to have it shipped back to your destination. This removal preference is a business decision you will have to make but I highly recommend utilizing the latter option so that you can personally inspect the merchandise for damage. In some cases, upon personal inspection you will find that the product itself is not damaged only the individual product packaging is. An undamaged product can be repackaged, relabeled with a new (FNSKU), and shipped back to the Amazon Fulfilment Center ultimately returning the merchandise to your active purchasable inventory.

\*<u>Note:</u> When your individual product packaging is manufactured I recommend requesting your supplier to produce at least (50) extra units to keep aside for product returns that are deemed unfulfillable due to solely warranting new packaging as previously discussed.

If the reason the merchandise is deemed unfulfillable by Amazon's (FBA) warehouse staff is due to the product or its individual packaging incurring "Warehouse Damage" or "Distributor Damage" this means that Amazon is as fault as the impairment to the unit was caused either directly by the staff at the Amazon Fulfillment Center or in route to or from the customer via Amazon's courier service. In this scenario instead of opting to have the merchandise disposed of or shipped back to you I recommend requesting a refund from Amazon for the amount they reimbursed the customer from your account for their returned product with exception to the (FBA) pick, pack, and ship fee.

**<u>To Track Your (FBA) Product Returns, follow the instructional steps included with the labeled images below:</u>**

**<u>Step #1:</u>** Navigate to http://sellercentral.amazon.com from within the Google Chrome Web Browser and sign into your Amazon Seller Central account.

**<u>Step #2:</u>** Using your mouse, without clicking, scroll over the "Orders" icon located within the taskbar at the top of the Amazon Seller Central dashboard to generate a list of navigational task buttons:

**amazon** seller central ▷  Catalog  Inventory  Pricing  Orders  Advertising  Stores  Reports  Performance  Appstore  B2B

**<u>Step #3:</u>** Using your mouse, left-click and release on the "Manage Returns" navigational task button located within the generated list:

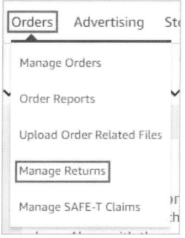

**<u>Step #4:</u>** Using your mouse, left-click and release on the small "View FBA Returns" icon located on the right-hand side of the "Manage Seller Fulfilled Returns" page:

View FBA Returns

❖ You have now been navigated to the "Manage FBA Returns" dashboard.

## From The "Manage FBA Returns" Dashboard You Can Track & Observe The Following List Of Items:

- Order ID Number (Customers Order #)
- Image Of The Product
- Products Name, (ASIN), Or (SKU)
- Customer Return Reason
- Return Authorized Date
- Customer Refund Date
- Unit Received Date
- Disposition
- Return Status
- Action

## To Individually Track & Manage Your Unfulfillable (FBA) Product Returns, follow the instructional steps included with the labeled images below:

**Step #1:** Navigate to http://sellercentral.amazon.com from within the Google Chrome Web Browser and sign into your Amazon Seller Central account.

**Step #2:** Using your mouse, without clicking, scroll over the "Inventory" icon located within the taskbar at the top of the Amazon Seller Central dashboard to generate a list of navigational task buttons:

**Step #3:** Using your mouse, left-click and release on the "Manage FBA Inventory" navigational task button located within the generated list:

❖ You have now been navigated to the "Manage FBA Inventory" dashboard.

**From The "Manage FBA Inventory" Dashboard You Can Track & Observe The Following List Of Items:**

- Status
- Image
- SKU (Condition)
- Product Name (ASIN)
- Date Created
- (FNSKU)
- Price +Shipping
- Inbound (Shipments)
- Available
- Unfulfillable
- Reserved
- Fee Preview (Storage)

**Step #4:** Locate the "Unfulfillable" column:

**Unfulfillable**

**Step #5:** Using your mouse, left-click and release on the blue "Unfulfillable" icon which will highlight in orange and bring all of your unfulfillable products to the top of your inventory list:

Unfulfillable ▼

**Step #6:** As you sort through your inventory list if you have unsellable merchandise you will be able to observe a red number in the "Unfulfillable" column which indicates the number of units for that particular (SKU) that are unsellable. If you do not have unsellable merchandise you will not observe a number in the "Unfulfillable" column thus requiring no action.

**Step #7:** Using your mouse, left-click and on the red number within the "Unfulfillable" column to generate an explanation and request removal task button.

**Step #8:** As you can observe in the screenshot below, the disposition will be clearly stated, which will determine your required removal action as previously discussed. In this case, the product has been deemed "Customer Damaged" by the (FBA) warehouse staff thus this merchandise requires removal from the Amazon Fulfilment Center. Using your mouse, left-click and release on the "Submit" navigational task button to "Create a removal order" for this product:

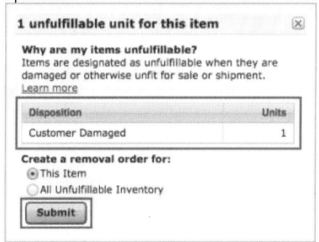

*Note:** When Amazon is at fault due to the product return being deemed unfulfillable due to "Warehouse Damage" or "Distributor Damage" Amazon will typically automatically reimburse you for the merchandise and notify you of this action by utilization of a notification sent to your email but please be aware that this is not always the case. In scenarios where they do not automatically reimburse or contact you regarding your unfulfillable "Warehouse Damaged" or "Distributor Damaged" merchandise it will be your responsibility to contact Amazon directly to request a reimbursement for the product.

**To Request A Reimbursement From Amazon For Your Unfulfillable (FBA) Product Returns Deemed "Warehouse Damaged" or "Distributor Damaged", follow the instructional steps included with the labeled images below:**

**Step #1:** Navigate to http://sellercentral.amazon.com from within the Google Chrome Web Browser and sign into your Amazon Seller Central account.

**Step #2:** Using your mouse, left-click and release on the "Help" icon located on the top right-hand side of the Amazon Seller Central dashboard to navigate to the "Help for Amazon Sellers" page:

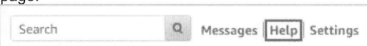

**Step #3:** Using your mouse, left-click and release on the "Contact Seller Support" navigational task button located on the right-hand side of the page to generate a list of actions:

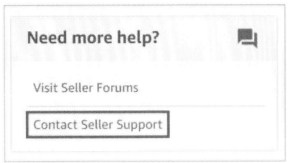

**Step #4:** Using your mouse, left-click and release on the "Browse more solutions for new sellers" navigational task button from within the generated list of actions:

Browse more solutions for new sellers >

**Step #5:** Using your mouse, left-click and release on the "Can't find what you need" navigational task button to generate a list of actions:

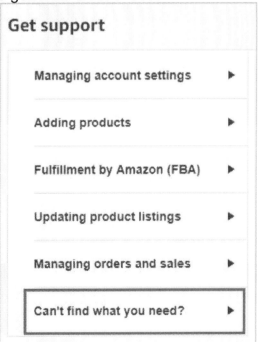

**Step #6:** Using your mouse, left-click and release on the "Contact Us" navigational task button from within the generated list of actions:

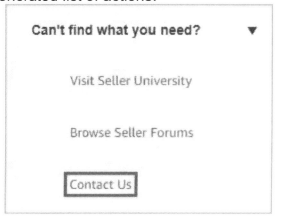

**Step #7:** Using your mouse, left click and release on the "Selling on Amazon" navigational task button:

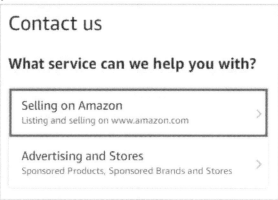

**Step #8:** Using your mouse, left-click and release on the "Fulfillment by Amazon" navigational task button to generate a list of actions:

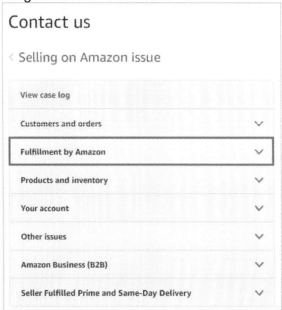

**Step #9:** Using your mouse, left-click and release on the "Inventory Damaged or Inventory Lost in Warehouse" navigational task button from within the generated list of actions:

**Step #10:** Using your mouse, left-click and release on the "Investigate Inventory Damaged in FBA Warehouse" navigational task button located in the center of the screen:

### What kind of issue are you having?
○ Investigate Inventory Lost in FBA Warehouse
○ Investigate Inventory Damaged in FBA Warehouse

**Step #11:** Describe your issue, such as I have within the screenshot below, and then enter the "Transaction ID" number for the order you are requiring reimbursement:

**Step #12:** Using your mouse, left-click and release on the "Send" button to complete your request for reimbursement notification to Amazon:

**Step #13:** Wait for a response and action to be taken by Amazon in regard to your request for reimbursement.

*Note: To avoid individually tracking and managing your unfulfillable (FBA) product returns you can opt to automatically have Amazon either dispose of or ship your unfulfillable merchandise back to you. If you would prefer to utilize this method in contrast to individually managing your unfulfillable inventory refer to the following tutorial.

**To Automate The Management Of Your Unfulfillable (FBA) Product Returns, follow the instructional steps included with the labeled images below:**

**Step #1:** Navigate to http://sellercentral.amazon.com from within the Google Chrome Web Browser and sign into your Amazon Seller Central account.

**Step #2:** Using your mouse, without clicking, scroll over the "Settings" icon located on the top right-hand side of the Amazon Seller Central dashboard to generate a list of navigational task buttons:

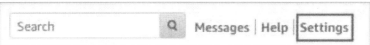

**Step #3:** Using your mouse, left-click and release on the "Fulfillment by Amazon" navigational task button located within the generated list:

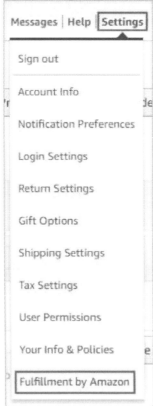

**Step #4:** Using your mouse, scroll down the page until you locate the section titled:

**Automated Unfulfillable Removal Settings**

**Step #5:** Using your mouse, left-click and release on the "Edit" navigational task button located on the right-hand side of the "Automated Unfulfillable Removal Settings" section:

Edit

**Step #6:** Using your mouse, left-click and release on the "Enable" navigational icon to check the box:

**Automated Unfulfillable Removal Settings**

Automated Unfulfillable Removals:    ○ Enable
Learn more    ● Disable

**Step #7:** Using your mouse, left-click and release on either the "Return" or "Dispose" icon to automate the process for all unfilled product returns. You will then schedule the time you wish this occur (Weekly, Twice a month, Or Once a month). If you are opting to have your merchandise returned to your destination in contrast to being disposed of be sure to fill out the informational boxes provided (Name, Address, and Phone Number):

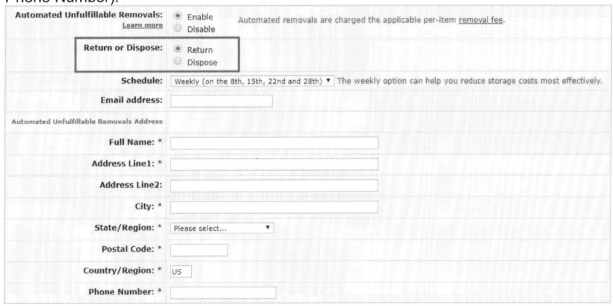

**Step #8:** Using your mouse, left-click and release on the "Update" button to finish automating your unfillable product removal:

Update

## Pro Tip:

- For each product listing you create and manage that is fulfilled via (FBA) I recommend utilizing Helium 10's reimbursement assistance tool Refund Genie as was discussed in Chapter 4.

### (FBM) Product Return Policies & Management For Amazon Sellers:

When utilizing (FBM) as your product fulfilment method Amazon requires you to adhere to their return policy by offering the customers the opportunity to return their merchandise in exchange for a refund for at least (30) days post purchase. It is your responsibility to elect an address for your merchandise to be sent to when a customer chooses to return their order in exchange for a refund. When your returned merchandise arrives back to your designated address you will utilize your Amazon Seller Central account to promptly authorize a reimbursement of funds to the buyer for their purchase. The customer must be reimbursed for their order within (2) business days post product return receival at your facilities. If you fail to refund the customer within the allotted time Amazon may issue the reimbursement on your behalf and take the order amount out of your funds. Although there are other options available I recommend operating your business with a 100% customer satisfaction mentality by offering a prepaid return shipping label and a full refund to all customers who opt to return their order regardless of the reason they are returning the merchandise. By operating your business in this manner, you will keep both your reputation with your consumers and Amazon healthy. Furthermore, you will avoid having an Amazon A-z Guarantee claim brought forth by a customer against your Amazon Marketplace business practices which could be detrimental to your reputation with Amazon and result in Seller Central account suspension.

When you receive your returned merchandise, I recommend personally inspecting it for damage. Upon personal inspection you can determine whether the product has incurred damages and whether or not it is sellable. If the merchandise is in perfect working order and pristine condition you can add the item back to your active purchasable inventory. Furthermore, in certain cases you may observe that the product itself is not damaged only the individual product packaging is. In this scenario, you will repackage the merchandise in new packaging and add the item back to your active sellable inventory.

*Note: When your individual product packaging is manufactured I recommend requesting your supplier to produce at least (50) extra units to keep aside for product returns that are deemed unfulfillable due to solely warranting new packaging as previously discussed.

**To Elect A Product Return Address, follow the instructional steps included with the labeled images below:**

**Step #1:** Navigate to http://sellercentral.amazon.com from within the Google Chrome Web Browser and sign into your Amazon Seller Central account.

**Step #2:** Using your mouse, without clicking, scroll over the "Settings" icon located on the top right-hand side of the Amazon Seller Central dashboard to generate a list of navigational task buttons:

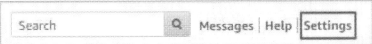

**Step #3:** Using your mouse, left-click and release on the "Return Settings" navigational task button located within the generated list:

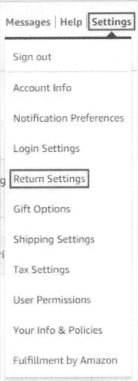

**Step #4:** Using your mouse, left-click and release on the "Return Address Settings" navigational task button:

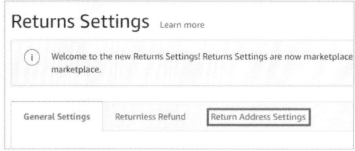

**Step #5:** Using your mouse, left-click and release on the "Set the address" navigational task button:

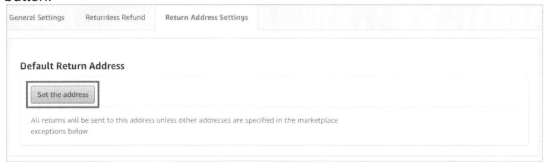

**Step #6:** Using your mouse, left-click and release on the "Manage your return address" navigational task button:

**Step #7:** Using your mouse, left-click and release on the "Add new address" navigational task button:

**Step #8:** Title your address for easy memorable access from your Amazon Seller Central account and then add your desired product return address information. Then using your mouse, left-click and release on the "Add address" navigational task button:

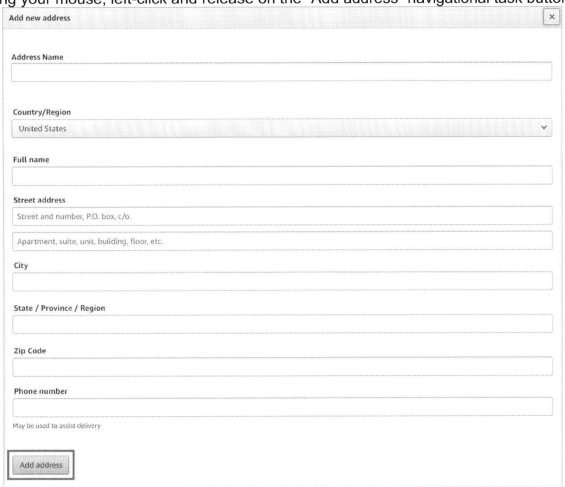

**Step #9:** Using your mouse, left-click and release on the "Set the address" navigational task button:

**Step #10:** Choose your newly create address from the list utilizing the check box. Then using your mouse, left-click and release on the "Use this address" icon to complete the process:

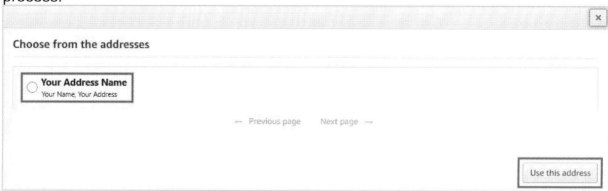

❖ You have now elected your desired product return address.

## To Edit Your (FBM) Product Return Preferences, follow the instructional steps included with the labeled images below:

**Step #1:** Navigate to http://sellercentral.amazon.com from within the Google Chrome Web Browser and sign into your Amazon Seller Central account.

**Step #2:** Using your mouse, without clicking, scroll over the "Settings" icon located on the top right-hand side of the Amazon Seller Central dashboard to generate a list of navigational task buttons:

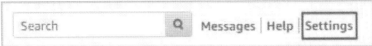

**Step #3:** Using your mouse, left-click and release on the "Return Settings" navigational task button located within the generated list:

❖ You have now been navigated to your "Return Settings" page where you can set your product return preferences. I recommend scrolling through the page and choosing the options that best suit your business needs.

*Note: If you have any questions when choosing your return preferences, you can utilize the "Learn More" icon located on the right-hand side of the "Return Settings" title:

## To Manage Your (FBM) Product Returns, follow the instructional steps included with the labeled images below:

**Step #1:** Navigate to http://sellercentral.amazon.com from within the Google Chrome Web Browser and sign into your Amazon Seller Central account.

**Step #2:** Using your mouse, without clicking, scroll over the "Orders" icon located within the taskbar at the top of the Amazon Seller Central dashboard to generate a list of navigational task buttons:

**Step #3:** Using your mouse, left-click and release on the "Manage Returns" navigational task button located within the generated list:

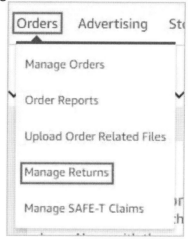

❖ As you can observe form the screenshot below you have now been navigated to the "Manage Seller Fulfilled Returns" page:

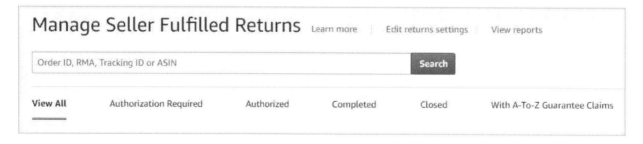

**To Issue A Full Refund To A Customer For An (FBM) Product Return, follow the instructional steps included with the labeled images below:**

**Step #1:** Navigate to http://sellercentral.amazon.com from within the Google Chrome Web Browser and sign into your Amazon Seller Central account.

**Step #2:** Using your mouse, without clicking, scroll over the "Orders" icon located within the taskbar at the top of the Amazon Seller Central dashboard to generate a list of navigational task buttons:

**amazon** seller central    ▷    Catalog    Inventory    Pricing    [Orders]    Advertising    Stores    Reports    Performance    Appstore    B2B

**Step #3:** Using your mouse, left-click and release on the "Manage Orders" navigational task button located within the generated list:

❖ You have now been navigated to "Manage Orders" section of your Amazon Seller Central account.

**Step #4:** Locate the customer order that requires a refund.

**Step #5:** From within the "Action" column, using your mouse, left-click and release on the "Refund order" navigational task button:

**Step #6:** On the "Refund order" page:

     **1)** Using your mouse, left-click on the box titled "Refund full amount."
     **2)** Select the reason for the refund.
     **3)** Add a Memo to the buyer (Optional).

**Step #7:** Using your mouse, left-click and release on the "Submit refund" to complete the reimbursement process.

## How To Utilize Product Returns To Your Advantage:

In certain scenarios, product returns can be a helpful tool that you can utilize to gain insight into what you are doing wrong and what could be changed to make your product better. For example, if numerous customers are complaining within their product reviews or directly to you within your message center that a certain aspect of your merchandise is easily breakable therefore resulting in product returns you could opt to have it manufactured with a more durable type of material on your next mass order from your supplier. You could then opt to state the fact that you improved the merchandise directly on your product listing.

## Properly Handling (FBM) Product Replacement Requests:

In certain scenarios, when utilizing (FBM) the customer may receive a product that incurred damage during the shipping process and will request that a replacement unit of the same merchandise be shipped to them instead of opting to return the item in exchange for a refund. In this type of situation, although there are other options available, I recommend offering the customer a prepaid shipping label so that they can return the damaged merchandise to your elected address. Once you receive the returned product you will then promptly ship them a new order to their designated address in exchange for the old the unit. Some Amazon Sellers prefer to ship the customer a replacement unit without requiring the return of the damage merchandise. I do not recommend utilizing the replacement without return method due to the fact that some crafty buyers may be simply attempting to receive free merchandise when requesting a replacement order. Although you will still be required to ship the consumer a new unit regardless of whether or not the product truly incurred damage at least you have the opportunity to personally inspect it. Upon personal inspection you can determine whether the merchandise has actually incurred damages and whether or not it is sellable. If the product is in perfect working order and pristine condition you can add the item back to your active purchasable inventory.

*Understanding how to properly handle product returns is another significant essential milestone to becoming and remaining a successful Amazon Seller.

# Chapter 20:

## How To Handle Amazon Seller Central Account Suspension & Revoked Seller Privileges:

If the event that you encounter the unfortunate scenario of having your Amazon Seller account suspended and your selling privileges revoked due to unintentionally violating Amazon's (TOS) or not adhering to Amazon's policies regarding account health performance metrics do not be discouraged. Depending on the severity of the problem, the issue is typically temporary and can be resolved through providing a (POA) Plan Of Action document correspondence with Amazon's Seller Performance Team. Your (POA) document should contain a brief proper apology where you accept full responsibility for the incident, a short excerpt stating that you understand Amazon's (TOS) regarding the specific problem, an acknowledgement that you comprehend why your Amazon Seller privileges have been revoked, an explanation of why the occurrence happened, an outlined description of the exact steps you will take to address the current issue, and techniques you will utilize to prevent this situation from occurring again in the future. When you write your (POA) do so in a professional, clear, concise, and knowledgeable manner that directly addresses the issues that lead to the suspension.

**To Submit A (POA) To Amazon's Seller Support Team & Get Your Amazon Seller Privileges Reinstated, follow the instructional steps included with the labeled images below:**

**Step #1:** Navigate to http://sellercentral.amazon.com from within the Google Chrome Web Browser and sign into your Amazon Seller Central account.

**Step #2:** Using your mouse, without clicking, scroll over the "Performance" icon located within the taskbar at the top of the Amazon Seller Central dashboard to generate a list of navigational task buttons:

**Step #3:** Using your mouse, left-click and release on the "Account Health" navigational task button located within the generated list:

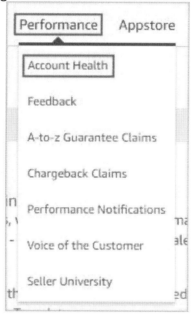

**Step #4:** Using your mouse, left-click and release on the "Reactivate your account" navigational task button to launch the (POA) document.

**Step #5:** Complete the Amazon provided (POA) document utilizing the techniques and suggested guidance discussed above.

**Step #6:** Once you have finished the (POA) document you will utilize the "Submit" task button to send the official form to Amazon's Seller Performance Team for review.

**Step #7:** Periodically check your email and look for a response from Amazon regarding your Amazon Seller privilege reinstatement appeal.

**OR:**

❖ Locate the "Submit Appeal" navigational task button located within the initial email you received regarding your account suspension and revoked seller privileges. The "Submit Appeal" button will navigate you directly to the (POA) document.

*Understanding how to properly handle Amazon Seller Central account suspension and revoked seller privileges is a preventive essential milestone to remaining a successful Amazon Seller.

# Pro Tips:

## Pro Tip #1:

When you are first starting out as an Amazon Seller, depending on your total investment amount, I recommend beginning by designing (1) brand that retails (1) or (2) types of products. I suggest this low amount due to the fact that retailing merchandise on the Amazon Marketplace is costly and quite a learning experience. As you perform the various tasks involved with being an Amazon Seller you will become familiar with the process and you will acquire the necessary knowledge required to successfully expand your current brand to include new types of merchandise. Once you obtain the skill set required to create, market, and sell one brand you can then opt to utilize your experience to fluidly design new brands and exponentially grow your company.

## Pro Tip #2:

If you are experiencing a heavy volume of sales and your company begins to rapidly grow due to your success as an Amazon Seller you may become overwhelmed with the many tasks involved with operating a retail business on the Amazon Marketplace. If this scenario takes place it may be time to hire and train a few employees and slowly build a team to handle such tasks as customer service, inventory management, product photography, product discovery, product sourcing, product listing optimization, keyword research, product returns, personal product inspection on mass orders, and preparing (FBA) or (FBM) shipments.

## Pro Tip #3:

Utilize the following social media sites to create brand awareness and drive external traffic to your Amazon product listings and Amazon Storefronts to convert the consumers clicks into sales:

### Facebook:

If you do not already have one, I recommend creating a social media account on www.facebook.com. You can then utilize Facebook ad campaigns to market your merchandise to drive external traffic to your Amazon product listings and directly to your unique (URL) Amazon Storefront. To perform this task, once you create your Facebook account, I recommend downloading the mobile Facebook Ads manager app from the Google Play Store (Android Devices) or Apple App Store (Apple Devices) which allows you to create and design specifically target marketed ads for your Amazon product listings.

**Helpful Hint:**

To generate brand awareness, talk about the uniqueness of your merchandise, discuss key features of your products, gain company visibility outside of Amazon, and ultimately drive external customer traffic to your Amazon product listings or Amazon Storefront, I recommend utilizing your Facebook account to create a page specifically dedicated to your business a few months prior to your first product launch. You will then utilize your contacts within Facebook as well as join Facebook groups that may take a particular interest in your specific type of merchandise to produce a base of followers. You can then opt to discuss new products prior and post launch on Amazon. Furthermore, you can utilize your Facebook Business Page to distribute coupons for your Amazon product listings and discuss upcoming or current promotional deals you may be running for your product listings.

## YouTube:

I recommend creating and uploading videos to YouTube free of charge that showcases your company, brands, and the products you carry. The video can be used as a means of presenting your merchandise to your customers, advertising your website, marketing your Amazon Storefront, explaining your products usage, exhibiting your products in use, and talking about the history of your brands. Furthermore, you can utilize Google Ads formerly known as Google AdWords at www.ads.google.com to advertise your specific merchandise on Google and YouTube through utilization of paid market targeted ads.

## Pinterest:

If you do not already have one, I recommend creating a social media account on www.pinterest.com utilizing your primary company name and Web address. You can then utilize Pinterest to market your merchandise by uploading images of your products with hyperlinks to drive external traffic to your company website, Amazon product listings, and directly to your unique (URL) Amazon Storefront.

**Pro Tip #4:** As you become successful as an Amazon Seller you could opt to dedicate some of the financial resources you procure to researching, locating, and contacting a celebrity or athlete to endorse the brands you create. Utilization of this marketing tactic can give your brand added integrity, strengthen your brand's image, significantly increase your brand's visibility, create an immense amount of brand awareness, generate a newfound customer following, and ultimately increase your overall sales volume. Although some celebrities or athletes may be difficult to connect with directly you can typically locate their agent's contact information online. Upon initial contact with their agent you can discuss the endorsement of your brand and the cost of doing so.

**Pro Tip #5:** Remember to prepare and file your company's annual Federal and State taxes in your country residence.

**Pro Tip #6:** I recommend paying close attention to Amazon's news feed within your Amazon Seller Central account for informative updates made to the Amazon Marketplace as well as potential changes in Amazon's third-party seller (TOS). Furthermore, due to Amazon regularly updating their (TOS), I suggest reviewing each aspect of Amazon's (TOS) on a quarterly basis to identify possible applicable guideline revisions or changes that could directly affect your businesses operations, such as alterations to their customer review policies, consumer communication guidelines, Seller Feedback rules, (FBA) shipment receival instructions, and cost of (FBA) fees.

**Pro Tip #7:**

If you have done everything in your power to properly utilize the various tactics in this book to retail your merchandise on the Amazon Marketplace yet you are experiencing an extreme lack of sales volume then it may be time to resolve the issue by having your entire stock of problematic merchandise shipped back to you from the Amazon Product Fulfillment Center (FBA Only), permanently deleting the product listing, attempting to regain your initial investment by retailing your remaining stock singly or wholesale on another online marketplace platform, such as eBay or AliExpress, and discovering a different type of merchandise to sell on Amazon, ultimately starting afresh.

# Looking Forward To The Future:

If the brands you build and the products you retail on Amazon become tremendously popular you may receive an invite directly from Amazon to become a first-party seller. This would allow you access to Amazon Vendor Central where you would become a product supplier for Amazon in contrast to solely retailing merchandise to their customer base as a third-party seller.

If you discover a profitable product idea, design it well, manufacture it with high-quality materials, and add the perfect essential features you could potentially expand your business ventures outside of Amazon by entering into the brick and mortar market. Retailing your merchandise in establishments, such as Target, will result in greater audience reach, wider scope of brand visibility, and an influx of substantial financial gain.

Becoming fluent in the art of discovering viable profitable merchandise to sell and expert brand builder can lead to being able to retail your created brands and product designs to large companies for a hefty financial gain. Ultimately, you could build a business whose sole operation is focused on discovering product ideas, designing merchandise, building brands, creating enterprises, and then selling those concepts to wealthy notable companies.

# Conclusion:

I truly hope that "The Official Amazon Seller Classroom In A Book Volumes I, II, III" have exceeded your expectations, that you found them informative, and that the lessons within significantly accommodate you in your Amazon focused e-commerce ventures. I sincerely wish you the very best of luck in forming an exceptional company and finding great success as an Amazon Seller. Building a prosperous business takes knowledge, familiarity, time, and patience. Try to remember to always remain confident, optimistic, and persistent in your pursuits. Furthermore, be sure to plan ahead, give yourself credit when due, rest when you need it, celebrate when things go right, and never give up.

❖ Furthermore, if you require instructional assistance on how to optimally utilize social media outlets as an Amazon Seller I will be releasing an e-book on Kindle & Nook regarding this topic on 10/01/2020. The publication will contain a comprehensive informative step-by-step guide with included tutorials that teach you how to efficiently utilize social media outlets, such as Facebook, YouTube, Instagram, Twitter, and Pinterest to effectively drive external traffic directly to your Amazon product listings.

# FREE GIFT: One-On-One (5) Question Live Email Business Consultation With The Author:

If you require additional instructional assistance in regard to the information in this book, necessitate further guidance on any aspect of being an Amazon Seller, or have general inquiries about starting a company and building a business be sure to personally email me your list of questions at the address provided below.

### Eligibility Requirements, Criteria, Policies, & Email Address:

### PROOF OF PURCHASE:

- In Order To Receive The Free Gift, Purchase Of "The Official Amazon Seller Classroom In A Book: Volumes I, II, & III" Is Required.
- Date Of Purchases For Volume I, II, & III Are Required & Must Be Sent With The Initial Email Containing Your Questions To Verify Your Order.
- Amazon Transaction Order #'s For Your Purchases Of "The Official Amazon Seller Classroom In A Book" Volumes I, II, & III Are Required & Must Be Sent With The Initial Email Containing Your Questions To Verify Your Order.

### Criteria:

- (5) Question Maximum Limit Per Proof Of Purchase
- Questions Must be Received In An Organized Numbered (1-5) List Format

### Policy:

- (1) Redemption Per Verified Proof Of Purchases

### Email Questions To The Provided Address Below:

- officialamzseller@gmail.com

Printed in Great Britain
by Amazon